A LOUD APPEAL

A LOUD APPEAL

Andrew Wingfield Digby

HODDER AND STOUGHTON
LONDON SYDNEY AUCKLAND TORONTO

British Library Cataloguing in Publication Data

Digby, Andrew Wingfield
    A loud appeal.
    1. Christian life
    I. Title
    248.4

    ISBN 0 340 42336 6

Hodder and Stoughton Editorial Office: 47 Bedford Square, London WC1B 3DP.

Contents

Foreword

According to my scrap-book ("Disasters of this world") a bloke called Wingfield Digby clean bowled me in 1976. If my memory is to be relied upon, the ball was a long hop which shot along the ground to hit off stump as I attempted the pull stroke. If Digby's memory is to be relied upon, the ball was cunningly flighted, dipped at the last moment, cut back sharply and beat the batsman all ends up – a masterful delivery.

We met again, on the field, in 1986. By this time Digby had finished all of his degree courses and, there being none left in the books, had entered the world. Despite his age, he was chosen to play for Dorset against Somerset at the County Ground. This time I managed to edge the ball, only to be caught at slip (as opposed to "in the slips" – Digby is not so recklessly optimistic as to have "slips"). We had had a bit of a duel already, with Digby wobbling the ball in the air and Roebuck being lucky to survive. This, at least, was Digby's interpretation of events. Repeatedly he stared at the heavens as if to complain that the gods (sorry, I suppose in his case we'd better say the God) are not just. Digby bowls rather as Fred Trueman used to, in a way that suggests that if all is right with the world a wicket will fall every ball. It is "these late eclipses in the sun and moon" which exasperate him, those and the umpires whom he often finds to be men of stone.

We had played in the same team, the Combined Oxford and Cambridge Universities XI, most memorably in Barnsley where the poor man on the loudspeaker had to announce that one R. le Q. Savage was bowling to our

Barry Leadbeater at one end, while Andrew Wingfield Digby was bowling to our Alan Ramage at the other end. Yorkshire never really had a chance. After the game, Boycott, who had been injured, appeared in our room to say that when he had wished us luck he hadn't meant "that much bloody luck".

Digby took 2 wickets in his first over in Barnsley. Once he dismissed Eddie Barlow first ball, and throughout his cricketing career he has, as Alan Gibson has written, "moved in a mysterious way, and taken some wickets". His action belied a cunning aspect, a competitive streak and a command of movement. He was, in short, a pretty good bowler. If 1986 is anything to go by, he still is.

Andrew and I have met many times away from cricket's fevered brow. At a time when sport is lurching towards hysteria he has recognised the need to remind sportsmen of things beyond the field, so that they are not swallowed up by their sports and do not sacrifice their values as they fight to succeed. Few activities take men up to the clouds and then down to the inferno as quickly and as unpredictably as sport. Some players, seeking to master themselves, have turned to psychologists for help. We are surrounded in our performances by people talking about champion factors. Most of them are charlatans. Proper psychologists do not rant or rave, rather they offer support and quiet words of encouragement. They recognise that sportsmen are let down not by themselves but by the elusive nature of their sport. Moreover, they recognise that many sportsmen blame themselves for their failures, not realising that a bad patch in cricket has more to do with a poorly played off-drive than a decline in character.

A few players listen to the words of these psychologists. Lots, perhaps advisedly, forget about the whole thing with pints of best bitter, rising the next morning refreshed and ready for the fray. One or two, sadly, turn to drugs, not for inspiration, not even for solace, but to counter the most dangerous threat of all – boredom. At first a career in sport fills a man's every need, sways him along with its adventure. Maturity, failure and success – the harsh experiences – harden the player until he realises the game is not enough.

Whichever way the player turns he hopes to find light and hope. An idealistic or analytical player will want to find answers technically, psychologically and mentally. Since leaving Oxford University Andrew Wingfield Digby has dedicated his life to offering the players a chance to turn to God not merely in their hour of need but as a way of life. Having experience there, he has understood the vulnerability of sport, has identified a need among players for something beyond their hazardous careers. He does not force himself or his faith on cricketers. It is something to which they can turn if they choose. He believes, and I think he is right, that every county club should have a chaplain, just as every club has a doctor and a physiotherapist. Sportsmen, and particularly those who play cricket (a game which because its sudden moment of wonder draws to it men who are particularly vulnerable to its sharp changes), are in need of mental and special care. It is not enough to offer bandages to men who risk success and failure, suitably stated in newspapers, every day of their lives.

In this book Andrew cheerfully recalls his curious career in cricket, and he reflects upon his effort to bring professional sportsmen to Christianity. In this work he will help many and harm none. I like particularly the story about Andrew's arriving in a down-and-out place in London, breezing through the door, rushing eagerly up to the girl in charge and announcing, "I'm Andrew Wingfield Digby and I'm here to help." Vic Marks passed the story on to me (years ago) and we both like it because it caught so much of Andrew's character – an intrepid spirit, bright optimism, a want of cynicism and a willingness to rush in. At once everyone knew that Andrew meant well, was prepared to work and was a trifle naïve.

Time has brought sensitivity, and has not dampened the spirit.

Good luck with the book and good luck with the work.

Peter Roebuck
Somerset County Cricket Club

Introduction

Loosening up

This is a book for people who like sport. Quite honestly, if sport bores you don't buy it, and don't read on. My sport is cricket, so if you like that prince of games you will enjoy this book. But it is for all sportspeople, too.

Sport has always been very important in my life and a source of great pleasure . . . but it is not all-important and it does not give me the greatest pleasure. I explain what does in the book. I have tried to write a book explaining the Christian faith in a way which sportsmen and women will appreciate. Someone said to me the other day that I have a low laughter threshold, and I think that's true. There are many funny things in the world, and I hope that readers of my book will be entertained. But I hope also that you will be challenged and stimulated. There are a lot of laughs in sport and in life, but there is seriousness, too, and the main thrust of this book is deeply serious – a matter of life and death, you might say.

I hope that whatever happens you read my last two chapters where I explain the Loud Appeal.

I have been conscious of two great pitfalls as I have been writing and I hope I have avoided them.

I was aware that some people, indeed some sportspeople, regard the world of sport, especially international sport, as very glamorous and exciting. They even ascribe some importance to it in itself. The great performers seem larger than life, and their deeds and misdeeds hit the headlines. As a youngster I had this view of sport. I had the photograph of a Pakistani Test team in my bedroom – goodness knows why it was Pakistan – and attributed great importance to these men. I had my sporting heroes like many youngsters do, and I idolised them.

I have now been working with sport for a number of years and know its seamier side. It is no different and certainly no more important than many other facets of modern life. Good footballers and athletes bleed and weep like ordinary mortals. In writing a book about sport I am under no illusions, I hope, about sport, and I neither wish to elevate its importance, nor lift the lid on the can of worms it contains. It is simply the part of life in which I work and for which I have a deep concern.

Second, I was aware that some people might think that I am cashing in on the "big names" of sport and accuse me of name-dropping. Such books have been written. I have told the stories of many individuals, but I hope that it has been done only to illustrate the importance of the one name which is above every name.

I am grateful to many people and want to acknowledge some of them: the national executive of Christians in Sport encouraged me to write the book and gave me the time to do it. In return all the royalties (if there are any!) I shall contribute to the growth of the Christians in Sport ministry; Peter Roebuck's Foreword amused and encouraged me. It arrived on my desk on the morning of one of the most momentous days in the history of Somerset County Cricket Club – the special general meeting at Shepton Mallett which decided Peter's future. I am grateful to him. Mary Baynes, Christians in Sport's hard-working secretary, not only typed the manuscript but proffered invaluable advice, some of which I took; I wrote the bulk of the manuscript while staying with my parents in their home at Sandbanks in Dorset. I am grateful to them for letting me spread paper all over the place. Sadly, my mother died peacefully and victoriously before the book was published. If this book is dedicated to anyone, it is to her – a very special Christian lady.

My wife, Sue, and the children keep my feet on the ground, and the staff and people of St Aldate's and St Matthew's churches in Oxford are a life-line to normal Christian experience. I am grateful to them all.

Andrew Wingfield Digby

1

Marking the Run-Up

The first major decision of my life had to be made in the summer of 1969. In a real sense this was the first crisis. The very fact that it was the first crisis or decision says a lot about the stability, comfort and security of my upbringing.

In the summer of 1969 there I was – an eighteen-year-old ex-public schoolboy about to go up to Oxford to read history, the youngest son of a West Country parson, passionately fond of rugger, cricket, fishing, shooting and most other things done out-of-doors – working in Jeyes's lavatory-paper factory in Plaistow, in the East End of London.

My job was in the waste-paper section (waste – not used). When the machines loaded with massive rolls of double-thick Babysoft broke down, literally yards and yards of paper would spill on to the floor. The "waste" ended up in my section where it had to be baled for recycling. My mate was an enormous coloured man, a bit like Chief in *One Flew Over the Cuckoo's Nest*. Incidentally, he maintained that he was a Red Indian and had flown jet planes during the Napoleonic wars!

I discovered with his assistance that I could completely hide under the waste paper and listen undisturbed by the "gaffer" to as many hours of Test Match commentaries as the BBC would broadcast. John Arlott was even more mellow ten feet under a pile of Babysoft. Occasionally, work, or my other mate – a globe-trotting hippy – would intervene. The former to collect more paper from the broken-down machines, the latter to suggest we sneak out to the pub for a pint.

In this unpromising environment, I committed my life to Christ.

Sherborne

Dad was the vicar of Sherborne in Dorset throughout my formative years. We moved up the A30 to Salisbury at the end of 1968. Sherborne is my family's home-town, and a branch of the family has owned Sherborne Castle and the Digby estate since the seventeenth century.

We are a close family (I have two brothers and a sister) and life was fun, if largely uneventful. I suppose the parish had a somewhat sceptical view of the "vicarage boys". I managed to shoot my brother Nicholas in the leg with an air-gun, I recall, and more than one wedding couple had their chat with the vicar disturbed by a cricket ball flying through the window. Nick even threw a bat through the study window on one occasion!

Church was something we did – quite seriously really. We assumed that God was around, but gave Him very little thought. Life was totally dominated in teenage years by pursuits of the sports we all loved and as many of the girls from the girls' school as we could lay our hands on. Not that anything immoral took place. I was terribly shocked by the prevalent and increasing promiscuity of some of my contemporaries at Sherborne School, where I was a boarder. We were '60s children, but the loving, protective, Christian atmosphere of our home cocooned us from the excesses, as we saw them, of those around us.

Life was about sport. In the winter I played rugger, never very well, but eventually made it into the 1st XV as stand-off half. The master in charge, former Somerset cricketer Micky Walford, said at the first training session of the term, "you had a raw deal with the cricket, old boy,

so you can play every game in the 1st XV". I never scored
a point all term, but he kept his word.

It is perhaps worth recording my school cricket career.
In my penultimate season (1967) I played a few games for
the 1st XI. The first match was against the Dorset
Rangers, a team of engaging Dorset characters, strengthened by a few Dorset county players.

I have an endearing but somewhat eccentric cousin
Michael, who was due to open the innings for the
Rangers. I was positioned at mid-on and the opening
batsmen had to walk past me on their way to the wicket.

"I don't know who this b**** is," whispered Mike, "but
I'm going to run him out."

Now you need to put yourself in my shoes: I was
young (sixteen), playing what for me was my first big
game, wondering how real cricketers played, and nervous.

Mike hit the first ball hard and straight at a fielder.
"Come on, Tom, Dick, Harry, whatever your name is . . .
run!"

Tom, Dick or Harry set off for a run. Mike did not. The
former was run out before he had faced a ball.

"That'll teach you!" shouted Mike again. Tom, Dick or
Harry retired to the pavilion muttering unprintable
oaths. "So this is sport," I must have thought. After a few
games I was dropped to the 2nd XI. I was an undisting-
uished middle-order batsman. In 1968, history repeated
itself, but I broke back into the side for the last two games
– as an opening bowler! My first serious spell had been as
a desperate measure in the House match final. I discovered then that bowling straight – even if that is all you
do – can earn rich rewards – in this case 6 wickets for 24
runs. But I do not recall getting a wicket for the 1st XI. If
M. J. K. Smith had known this when I bowled him for 2 in
the Oxford University Parks in 1971, my second first-
class wicket, he would have understood better why that
same cousin Michael leapt like a man possessed out of his
deckchair. Michael had bet me two bottles of champagne

that I wouldn't clean bowl M. J. K. – he was an England captain after all!

I always found the Easter term at school most irksome – we played hockey. As a left-handed batsman I found it difficult to hold the hockey stick correctly, although ironically I was beginning to play golf right-handed . . . well, hit a golf ball anyway. In my final term at school (Easter 1969) when I was head of school, I was sent off in a home cricket match for dangerous play – I had hit the ball into the local cemetery.

Of course chapel every morning and an hour-long chapel service on Sundays was compulsory in those days. I remember only a few of the distinguished men who came to preach. I was spellbound by Dick Lucas's Bible teaching, but as soon as he finished I could remember only his shining, rather yellow face – "Perhaps he's a Chinaman," I thought. Ronnie Selby-Wright, all the way from Scotland, impressed me deeply and we corresponded for a while. In recent years I have seen Ronnie again and still he has the gentle power of a man of God.

But it was David Sheppard whom I remember best of all. Nowadays, David is Bishop of Liverpool, and a public figure; a familiar face on BBC's "Question Time" and often to be heard on the "World at One", David is an Old Sherburnian too, but much more importantly, he played cricket for England. Here before me was a man who had played at Lord's and Sydney. He had faced the great West Indian fast bowlers, Hall and Griffith, and made centuries for England. Perhaps more than anything else, he was a friend of Colin Cowdrey, who had been my hero ever since I could remember. What in the world would make a man turn his back on everything I dreamed of in order to dress up in weird clothes and talk about God in a chapel full of uninterested schoolboys? I was baffled and awed.

Some time later my father arranged for me to see David with a view to my spending a few months at the

Mayflower Family Centre in Canning Town, where at that time David was the warden. We met at the girls' school – forbidden, holy ground – where David had been preaching that particular weekend. He told me about the Mayflower.

Right in the heart of the new high-rise East End was a beacon of Christian hope and caring. As a resident, which is what I was applying to become, I would live as part of the small community, headed by David and Grace Sheppard, and assist with the youth clubs which were held most evenings of the week. I should also be available as a general dog's-body when required.

"You are, of course, a committed Christian?" asked David with what I detected to be a suspicious tone. I must have blushed, panic seized me, "Y-y-yes," I lied. For in my heart I knew that whatever was involved in being a "committed Christian" – and I hadn't a clue what it was – I had not got it. That question remains a vivid memory. In a few seconds I had discovered that I was not a Christian and I was a liar!

The Mayflower

In April 1969 I set off from Salisbury station for Canning Town. You cannot imagine, unless you have been to a rural public school and grown up in a county like Dorset, how I felt as I walked past the recently collapsed skyscraper, Ronan Point, and through the concrete jungle of the East End of London. Later two friends from the Mayflower, Tom and Terry, were to come to Salisbury for a weekend. We lived in the Close in a lovely house. As they said good-bye on the station, Tom said, "Fanks, Andrew, but I can't stand all that bleedin' green." As I entered Cooper Street for the first time I missed the "green" very much.

I was a fish out of water. Everyone was very kind and seemed so, well, happy. For me it was traumatic. On my first evening, a girl – a Christian girl I later discovered – asked me who I was and why I had come. "Andrew Wingfield Digby," I replied in my best Prince Charles voice, "and I've come to help."

"Why don't you *!*!*! off home," she replied. I was staggered.

After a couple of weeks in a Social Security office, filing, I got the job at Jeyes. In the evening I helped at clubs and attended prayer and Bible-study groups. It was very busy and, much to my surprise, terrific fun. But what was getting to me was the realisation that the rest of the residents had a relationship with Jesus which was not my experience. They explained the Good News to me, as it had no doubt been explained many times before, but this time I listened. I must acknowledge my need of help, surrender my life to Jesus, and ask Him into my life to be my Saviour and Lord.

It sounded so easy, yet I couldn't even form the words in my mind. Though outwardly enjoying myself, I was in turmoil inside. Not until early June in the canteen of the factory, a day when my Red Indian friend was not around, did I bow my head over a plastic mug and say under my breath, "Lord Jesus, come into my life."

Immediately, I knew I really was a Christian. I could have answered David's question without hesitation. There had not been any blinding lights or heavenly thunderbolt. Outwardly my life probably changed very little. But from that day on I have just known that God is my friend. Because Jesus died on the cross for me I was forgiven for ignoring His love for so long. Because Jesus rose from the dead and was alive, He lived, by His Spirit in me. It was miraculous, incredible almost – but it was true. I understood very little, but I knew that much. It was an immense relief to have decided.

We played cricket that summer too. Canning Town CC – a member of which was D. S. Sheppard (Sussex and England) – played every week in West Ham Park. I began to learn to bowl. The wickets were atrocious, so straight bowling was all that was needed. I remember my good friend and fellow resident, Henry Pearson, fired a bouncer over the head of "Sam", the large West Indian London Transport batsman, who was promptly given out caught behind the wicket. Sam sat down. "It hit my *!*! ear," he shouted repeatedly as his team-mates carried him off. They never behaved like that on the Upper at Sherborne.

When I returned to Salisbury at the end of July, I don't suppose I seemed any different. There were changes, however – I read my Bible every day now and tried to pray. I thought going to church was important and not just a duty, and I really did want to tell people what Jesus meant to me.

In Canning Town I had been made aware that believing in God, going to church, and being English – even if you've got all three – do not make you a Christian. I had come to see that in all of us there is something wrong about which we can do nothing. Left to my own devices I simply did not measure up to the standard required by God and exemplified in Jesus. I needed forgiveness

for the past and help to live life the right way in the
future.

I met people who told me that Jesus really would make
all the difference. Of course, I believed most of it already,
but they had something about them I definitely lacked.
Only when I took the plunge, so to speak, launched out
and asked Him to take over my life did I begin to discover
what they were talking about.

I returned to the West Country to play cricket for the
Dorset under-19s – the start of a long and happy
association with Dorset cricket. In my heart I felt like a
different person, but it was not long before I began to
drift back to the old ways. I have often found this since.
To be a Christian when surrounded by fellow believers is
relatively easy. Even when things are difficult, one's
friends keep one going. In most sports, and certainly in
most of the Dorset teams I have played, I have been alone
as a firm, committed believer. There has never been open
hostility, but the constant pressure to compromise is
always there, and I have often failed.

While I was at the Mayflower I felt as if I was making
vital life-changing decisions . . . and I suppose I was. But
as I look back, twenty years on, it seems different. I
believe that God was in control all the time. I really
believe, and I do not wish to sound trite or pious, that
God was preparing me for the future. Without the
Mayflower would I have made the faith I grew up with
my own personal faith? Without Dorset cricket would I
have ever been able to understand the situations that
many sportspeople get themselves into?

I had come to believe in the sovereign, controlling God
who is described in the Bible. He really was in control all
the time.

No doubt all of us who are now involved in the
movement known as Christians in Sport could tell stories
of how God led us to be of use to Him. In my own case
God took what I know to be a limited talent or natural
ability and as I tried to live life His way, He multiplied it.

.

Oxford

Oxford was a two-innings affair for me!

Between 1969 and 1972 I was at Keble College, reading modern history and enjoying the social life which is very much part of being an undergraduate. In the vacations I attended, from time to time, Christian camps run at a public school in Dorset, in a lovely village called Iwerne Minster, by an organisation called Scripture Union, about which I knew nothing. They were élitist (not only did you have to attend a public school to go there but only certain public schools!), male only (much to my disappointment) and dominated by sport. I'm afraid I loved every minute of it. More importantly I learned, as many others have, the basics of Christian living and teaching; that it was in the person of Jesus Christ and particularly by His death on the cross, that God intervened in human affairs. It may have been 2,000 years ago, but it was decisive. I also learned that only by giving time to God each day, quietly reading the Bible and praying, could one's faith grow.

Back at Oxford I supported the Christian Union without ever getting very involved. I suppose, like many Christian students, I wanted the best of both worlds and kept a foot firmly in each, but to some extent I lost out on both. Even while plunging into the "pagan" delights of university life, I felt God's restraining hand, and yet my failure to live wholeheartedly for the Lord stunted my witness and growth as a Christian.

The tensions of this double life were most evident in my cricket.

In my first year, to my surprise, I played as an opening bowler for the Authentics (the University 2nd XI). I was little more than a line-and-length military, medium "have a bowl because no one else can" type of chap. Nevertheless, I took it seriously, practised very hard, and enjoyed every minute of it. We played several county

2nd XI teams and I still remember very vividly playing on my first county ground – Worcester – a lovely place.

In my second year, I did well in the pre-season trials and got picked to play Warwickshire in the opening game. I took 2 wickets in the only innings of a rain-affected match (including M. J. K. Smith as already recalled), so I was on my way. Against Hampshire, Warwickshire (later in the season) and the Free Foresters I took 5 wickets in an innings. I mention this only because it was such a surprise to me and probably everyone else. I really did not think I could bowl and yet people seemed to get out . . . it's been the same ever since!

My ego soared in the summer of 1971. I loved seeing my name in the papers, playing against household names, and being part of the team. We were a poor side by any estimation, but I hardly noticed that, so thrilling was it to be playing. It was all a great ego trip. I walked tall in Oxford, was secretary of Vincents – the exclusive University Sportsmen's Club – and on my way to winning a blue. I thought of little else. My political thought tutor, whom I never met because he insisted on noon tutorials, sent me despairing telegrams, but I ignored them all.

One highlight to which I looked forward was the game against Kent. Would Colin Cowdrey play? Would I meet him? Perhaps I might even bowl at him, but of course I could never get him out. The day of the Kent match arrived. It was raining. Cricket is a desperate game when it rains. We all assembled in the pavilion and drank coffee. Cowdrey was there, introducing himself to all of us, enquiring about us and our cricket. One of my team-mates whispered to me, "He's introduced himself to me three times . . . you'd think he knew my name by now!"

My great idol was flesh and blood, capable of inane behaviour. How easy it is for us to put sportspeople on a pedestal, to make them larger than life. Yet even the greatest are just like the rest of us. A few years later I played with Colin for the MCC against Oxford. I found myself batting with him, and managed to hit a four past cover point. As we met in the middle of the wicket, the great man put his hand on my shoulder and said, "I haven't seen a cover drive like that since I played against Graeme Pollock." As my knees knocked I knew I had forgiven him!

It rained for three days in the match against Kent. We never bowled a ball.

The Oxford cricket season builds up to a climax with the annual Varsity match at Lord's – a three-day game against our arch rivals, Cambridge. We drew the game by the skin of our teeth. I recall going in to bat on the first evening as night-watchman (usually I was number 10) which meant batting at 4 to protect the better batsmen for the morning. All term I had jokingly boasted to the team about how well I should bat if I could get in as night-watchman at Lords. It's a long way to the wicket from the changing-rooms at cricket's headquarters, and I was very nervous.

Phil Edmonds – who was to become an England bowler – was operating from the Nursery end. I took guard, trying to look casual, but really in utter turmoil. "Henri", as Edmonds is known in cricket, slipped in a quick one – it hit the middle stump before I played a shot. As I walked out I looked up at the Warner stand – there were only fifty or sixty people there, but I think half of them were members of my family! Getting back to the changing-room, full of anger and disappointment, I discovered my team-mates falling about laughing. Sport inflates the ego only to deflate it pretty quickly!

Nevertheless a tally of 32 first-class wickets, 59 in all for the season was a record to be pleased with.

Year three on a modern history course at Oxford is finals year, and in June – some three weeks before the Varsity match – all finalists are examined on eight terms of work . . . there are no exams between your first term and your ninth. Everybody has a lot of work to do, and if you have played university sport in the intervening period, there is a certain amount of catching up to be done.

I played a couple of three-day games at the beginning of term before settling down in the library. With finals over there was time for only one game in the Parks before the team was picked. Having failed to distinguish myself, I was omitted from the team – it still seems to me to have been a poor piece of selection!

I was totally demoralised. The evening after being told I had been dropped I went to a May Ball, a sumptuous affair held in the beautiful grounds of Christ Church College, with my girlfriend, Sue (now my wife and mother of our three children). The tickets had cost a lot of grant money, but I was very bad company and the evening was a disaster.

Sport, even for amateurs, can easily dominate our lives. I look back now and see that God was teaching me, through this experience, that no part of our lives, including our love of sport or involvement in it, must take priority over our love and commitment to Him. As an undergraduate I had fallen into the trap into which many others fall of keeping God out of my sports life. I had failed to marry the two together. Now I see something which is one of the main themes of this book, that we can be both a Christian and "in sport". God is investing spiritually in sporting talent. He wants His people to be witnesses for Him in sport by fulfilling their God-given talent, and bringing all of their lives under the Lordship of Jesus Christ.

Ordination

I learnt this lesson by being dropped from my team. For a couple of years I felt quite bitter about it. What had been a glorious ego trip had ended in failure and disappointment. *My* talent had not been recognised. Gradually, over those two years, I became more and more aware that I should investigate the possibility of going into full-time Christian work. There was no startling revelation or call. Indeed for both Sue (to whom I was then engaged) and myself, ordination seemed frightening. Even as I went to a selection conference in January 1974, I was hoping that they would turn me down! They didn't and in the autumn of that year we found ourselves married and members of Wycliffe Hall, Oxford, an Anglican theological college. I am still not quite sure how it all happened. I remember the Bishop of Salisbury, which was my sponsoring diocese, saying that we should go to Cambridge this time. I thought that I'd never take a wicket on the batting paradise of Fenners! But perhaps what swung it most of all was the presence of the Rev. Peter Southwell, senior tutor at Wycliffe, who years before on the way to the pub in Iwerne Minster had suggested I should be ordained.

Early in 1975 I had to face the question of whether to play cricket seriously again or acknowledge that those days were past. I recall kneeling beside my bed and giving my cricket to the Lord. Cricket was something very important to me, but I no longer wanted it to get in the way of my Christian discipleship.

I prayed, "I will play or not play as you want, Lord, and not as I want." It was hard to do that – a real battle – because it meant facing the very real prospect of not playing seriously again.

That was the risk I had to take in surrendering that part of my life to Him. I suggest that it is the same for every Christian. For some of us it will be sport, but for others it might be a relationship, an ambition, a plan, or whatever. But until we are prepared to let it all go – and let it go permanently – we keep God at arm's length. Many people are afraid that God will mess up their lives, stop them doing the things they like doing, and generally be a killjoy. I think, deep down, that is what I thought. How wrong I was! Yes, it will be hard at times to be a Christian, there will be things to give up, but I have learnt that nothing beats the joy and purpose and plain human happiness of being a Christian.

My decision – and what a crucial one it turned out to be – had been made; my future cricket was in God's hands. The university captain, Trevor Glover, asked me to winter nets. I went to see the college principal, a godly and, we thought, rather eccentric man, Jim Hickinbotham, to seek counsel and advice. I tried to explain that, though of course I should love to play university cricket again, it had ceased to be an obsession. I told him that in the past cricket had, I felt, stunted my development as a Christian, but I did not think that was the case any more. Without hesitation Jim advised me to play. "We haven't had a cricket blue for years," he exlaimed. "You must play." I felt God had given me back something that I had been prepared to sacrifice. He seemed really good and generous. I was thrilled that He had said yes to cricket. What if He had said no? Of course, it would have been hard, but I believe I could have accepted it.

And so the three years that coincided with the beginning of Christians in Sport in this country, and which have shaped my subsequent life, began. It is my firm belief that everything hinged on those ten minutes I spent beside my bed when I gave it all to Jesus.

2

First Steps

The early days

I was not in on the very beginning of Christians in Sport, and so I am indebted to Gerald Williams, the BBC TV tennis commentator, Harry Hughes and Alan Godson for their recollections of the very early days.

Gerald Williams recalls in his marvellous little book, *A Whole New Ball Game*, how he met Eddie Waxer, an American touring the world in a ministry to sportspeople. In the summer of 1974 Eddie was introduced by Gerald to Alan Godson, an Anglican vicar in Liverpool and former top-class rugby player. Alan had played for Cambridge University, Lancashire, Fylde and all stations in between and had also had an England trial before retiring from competitive rugby during his first curacy. Years before, Gerald and Alan had become friends and it was the most natural thing in the world for Gerald to introduce his new American friend to his favourite vicar. It was in Gerald's words "a meeting which was to have a great impact".

In those early days Eddie would fly backwards and forwards across the Atlantic seeking out Christian contacts in the British sporting world.

Eddie would go and see the managers of league football clubs and ask to meet the Christians in the squad. This had little result as at that time there were no committed Christians playing in the leagues, or at least none emerged. So Eddie tried the big well-known churches. At Millmead Baptist Church in Guildford he located Harry Hughes.

Harry remembers being invited to a men's dinner at Purley by Kenneth Frampton. Everything was new for this big burly ex-pro soccer player. For twenty-seven years his wife Joyce had been praying for him, but football was Harry's god. Then in 1973 through the witness of a blind Christian, Harry had come to faith in Christ. "Who is really blind, Harry?" he had asked. Twenty-seven years is a lot of prayer and the scales fell from Harry's eyes. But it was a very young Christian who went to Purley that evening and became one of the founders of Christians in Sport and one of our most universally loved members.

Harry's next appointment was at the Goring Hotel in Berkshire for lunch. The date was 23rd April, 1976. Although there had been a preliminary meeting the previous October, it was this meeting at Goring which effectively began Christians in Sport.

It's worth taking time to introduce the various characters who attended. Most were clergymen, including Alan Godson from Liverpool; John Kilford – a former professional soccer player; ex-olympic athletes, Martin Wimbolt Lewis and Tom Farrell; Harry Bloomfield from Wantage; Mike Pusey (chaplain to Aldershot FC); and his assistant, Derek Brown from Farnborough. The company was completed by Kenneth Frampton and his secretary, Caryl Browne-Constable; Dickie Dodds (former Essex cricketer); and, of course, Harry Hughes. The convener and chairman was Eddie Waxer. The first thing anybody would notice was that there was not a current sportsman among them, although many had enjoyed illustrious careers in the past. Gerald, of course, as a tennis journalist was "in sport", but, alas, by his own admission not yet a Christian.

The minutes of the meeting record that those who assembled that day heard some recordings of Christian athletes telling their life-stories at President Ford's

"Prayer Breakfast for Athletes" in Washington. Eddie apparently spoke briefly – explaining his ideas. A dinner was planned to coincide with Wimbledon, and all agreed to invite as many British sportsmen and sportswomen as possible to an evening in London which would promote "Christian fellowship in the sports world".

Thus Christians in Sport began. For a man like Harry, who was determined to live his life for the Christ he had so recently come to know, it was exciting. For the first time, sportsmen were acting together to promote a Christian presence and witness in British sport. Harry's two "gods" were, it seemed, not as incompatible as he had supposed.

Harry Hughes and Joe Brown

Many sportsmen and sportswomen are not exactly anti-Christian. They just cannot see any connection between their sport and all this talk of God. Harry Hughes had begun his footballing life in Burnley, got transferred to Chelsea, where he played only a game or two in the 1st XI, and then on to Bournemouth and finally Gillingham.

It was at Bournemouth, now married to Joyce and beginning a family, that he played the bulk of his league football. Also in the team was Joe Brown, later manager of Burnley and the youth development officer at Manchester United. Joe was already unashamed to be known as a Christian. Season after season, Harry and Joe played, changed and showered together. Joe's witness was consistent.

"I thought my influence on Harry was nil," recalls Joe. "My words seemed to be going over his head, really. He seemed so indifferent to what I had to say. He was the last one I thought I had been able to get through to." But Harry was taking notice.

"Look what Joe's done," he would tell Joyce, when he

found another little Christian booklet in his pocket when
he got home. The combination of the faithful witness of a
team-mate and the prayers of a faithful wife had their
effect. But it took the challenge of that blind Christian to
get stubborn old Harry to his knees.

In Guildford Harry was running a sports shop and
managing the local non-league side. A change in the
traffic system in the town centre meant his business had
to close down and gave him the chance to return to the
professional game. Harry and Joyce moved to Tottenham
to run the Spurs shop on Tottenham High Road.

Over the years I have been to see them many times,
and there's always a warm welcome. Joyce seems to have
trouble with my name and she will often say, "Hello,
Digby, I'll get Harry." Well, what's in a name?

I suppose Harry's a bit of an institution at White Hart
Lane now. The players trust him and enjoy his company.
Everyone knows that he and Joyce are Christians and
they respect them for it. For a while Harry's minister at
the local Baptist church was the club chaplain before
other duties became too pressing. But there's still a
Christian presence in the club. Players can see that sport
and "this talk of God" do meet, because they combine in
a man like Harry Hughes.

During 1986, the year of the World Cup in Mexico,
Harry and Joyce were encouraged to discover that
England and Tottenham footballer Glen Hoddle had
become a Christian. Glenn and his wife, Anne, who had
been a church-goer for a long time, had been influenced
by a Christian friend who prayed for Glenn when he
was injured and by singer Cliff Richard at a Christians
in Sport dinner. But it was a visit to the Holy Land
in the spring of 1986 which finally brought home to
Glenn the realisation that the Bible events had really
happened.

Now Glenn, Anne and their two daughters live in
Monte Carlo, where Glenn plays for Monaco. They are
quietly growing in their new faith.

Joe Brown and his wife, Connie, returned north and he became manager of second-division Burnley. Here the 2nd team coach, Dave Merrington – a notoriously hard man as a player – became a Christian, too. "Actually," says Joe, "it was easier for David to talk about his beliefs to the players because as the manager, I had to be slightly aloof, in a way."

After Burnley, Joe settled at Manchester United. He is a man with a servant heart – perhaps an unusual characteristic in professional sport. Let me illustrate what I mean.

In 1985, Christians in Sport's annual conference weekend was at Kinmel Hall in North Wales. Some 180 people were expected on the Friday evening . . . but due to an administrative error, for which I was largely responsible, we had no food on the premises. Joe and Connie rolled up their sleeves, and got on with the job. Deliveries arrived, food materialised from late-night supermarkets. Everybody got fed. All weekend Joe and Connie slaved away in the background, unbidden and largely unrecognised. They seemed as the Bible says to "count it all joy".

Joe and Harry and their wives are examples of two couples who have successfully combined life at the centre of a busy football club with full-blooded Christian commitment. It can be done.

First encounters

At one level the show was on the road. From April 1976 on, regular gatherings of sportsmen occurred. Dinners were held for three years in London, arranged to coincide with Wimbledon. Gradually a mailing list of those interested was assembled.

Meanwhile, Eddie Waxer continued his researches.

At St Aldate's Church in Oxford he met sports enthusiast and rector, Michael Green. While I was studying for ordination at Wycliffe Hall . . . (and playing cricket!) we began to attend St Aldate's as and when we could. A friendship began with Michael which was to be significant a few years later. Michael directed Eddie in my direction and I was confronted one day at Wycliffe by a small but athletic-looking American with a crew cut who introduced himself as "Eddie".

In conversation with him I began to see for the first time that sport, in my case cricket, was part of God's plan for my life. It wasn't primarily "for fun", but "for Him". He challenged me concerning my witness to the players. He made me see that God was enabling me as a sportsman to be in places and reach people whom other Christians could not.

He made me see that I should be identifying those members of my team who seemed interested in Christianity, praying for them and seeking every opportunity to bring them to Christ. In a way in which I had never done before he encouraged me to bring Jesus into my sport and use it for Him. I could be a Christian in Sport. I was excited.

Oxford SCF

My growing understanding of what it meant to be a Christian and a sportsman manifested itself in the formation of the Oxford Sportsmen's Christian Fellowship. After a few months we changed the name to Christians in Sport.

It so happened – the God of coincidences fixed it actually – that we had committed Christians strategically placed in university sports.

Tim Bryan was the captain of rugger. One evening he was loafing around in the college lodge when he was approached by a stranger.

"Do you want to come to the mission meeting?" he asked.

"Well, why not?" said Tim. "I've nothing better to do."

The stranger was the Rev. Bruce Gillingham, later to be a friend and colleague at St Aldate's Church. Bruce had been a sporting superstar at Sherborne School, two years ahead of me. He had played for three years in the 1st XI hockey, 1st XI cricket and 1st XV rugger teams. Sadly, as an undergraduate in Oxford, he suffered a detached retina in one eye, which prevented his fulfilling that schoolboy promise. Mind you, he's still a devastating opening bat in the interdiocesan clergy cricket competition – the *Church Times* Cup.

When he approached Tim, he was one of numerous young clergymen drafted in to assist with the tri-annual Christian Union University Mission. Together they went to hear an explanation of what being a Christian meant. Tim remembers very little of the contents of the address, but he knew that it was time to take a stand and in a simple prayer, he asked God to forgive him and invited Jesus into his life.

After his time at Oxford, Tim became a policeman. He played rugger for the Metropolitan Police (a notoriously physical team) and became their captain. He also played a bit for the Harlequins and the London division in an England trial. Like many of us, he did not always find it easy to combine Christian faith and life in sport. For him there was the problem of being a Christian policeman, too, with the moral dilemmas that arise in that capacity. But he never gave up his faith, and in due course met Liz, a lovely Christian girl, who became his wife. They live in South London and run the Christians in Sport group there.

Back in Oxford, Tony Roake was a football blue. A blue is awarded to those who play against Cambridge in the annual Varsity match. Unfortunately, theological study, the disciplined life of a priest in training, and a liking for ale had produced a thickening of the waistline, and despite gifted ball skills (so he tells me) he was not actually in the university side. But he was a link with the soccer scene. Tony and his wife, Jill, now live in Bournemouth, where he is a vicar and co-ordinates the Christians in Sport group there.

Chris Pouncey was a hockey blue and another fellow-student at Wycliffe. After working in Africa for a number of years, Chris married and now farms in North Devon.

Helen Bayley seemed to be a blue at almost everything at which a girl could be a blue. She quickly became known as the "bionic woman"! After university she moved into the world of sports promotion where under her married name of Day she has become an influential figure.

I don't think any of us were living very effective Christian lives in our sports teams. To be honest I don't think any of us saw sporting talent in a Christian context.

Recently I was speaking at a Christian Union meeting at a teacher training college, and a girl came up to me and said that she had decided that she would use her talent for singing only at Christian events. Did I think she was right? I had some sympathy. After all, it so happened that her talent had uses in church. She could sing in choirs and even do solos. But I asked her what I was to do with my cricketing talent.

I admit I have played cricket in church. I do it to illustrate that as a bat is necessary for cricket, so Jesus is for life! You may think that rather fanciful! My wife does, too. The last time I tried it, I essayed a cover drive, got an inside edge and hit the tennis-ball firmly into my daughter's face.

"Thank God it was your own daughter," someone shouted from the back of the church.

No, be it music, speaking or drama, making coffee, or sporting ability, or whatever, God makes us for a purpose. The New Testament says "Run with patience the particular race God has set before us" (Heb. 12:1, Living Bible). Every aspect of our lives – personality and physical attributes – can be used for Him. So, my young singer friend has a gift which enables her to sing with those who are not Christians and share God's love and the Good News of Christ with them. Those of us with sporting gifts have opportunity and a duty to explore that talent and use it for God's glory and the spreading of His Kingdom.

Meeting together as Christians in Sport week by week, we began to encourage one another, and our confidence in speaking about our faith in our teams increased. Some people were convinced, but mainly those who were previously secret or quiet believers began to align themselves publicly with Christianity.

Paul Fisher was the university wicket-keeper, and a very good one, too. He is a Roman Catholic and has always been a devoutly religious person. Paul attended our meetings from the first days and began, for the first time, to talk about what he believed with people to whom he could relate and whom he respected as fellow-sportsmen. He would say, I'm sure, that he became much firmer in his convictions, and much more extrovert in the expression of his love for Christ. Years later, in 1985, when he was a member of the Christians in Sport cricket team that went to India, he was only too glad to speak of his belief in Jesus to churches and schools.

Of course, there were plenty of laughs at those early meetings – there always are when Christian sportspeople get together. Both the university opening bowlers (David Gurr and Ken Siviter) attended the meetings. One week we decided to discuss what was legitimate on the field of play and what was not. So the rugby players invited us to consider the ethics of ear-biting, the footballers exchanged clichés about the professional foul, the lady hockey players said anything goes, and we cricketers debated the use of the bouncer.

This was the era of those great Australian pace twins, Lillee and Thompson (or as Eric Morecombe once said, "Lillian Thompson"). Now they could bowl bouncers. I was far too slow to consider it, though I did bowl a deadly long hop! Dave Gurr had genuine pace and could make even the best players take notice. Ken Siviter, despite possessing a formidable physique, was only quick when he bowled from 17 yards rather than the statutory 22. This he did about twice an over, much to the captain's annoyance.

Ken is a man of a few well-chosen words. He is the son of the former vicar of Knotty Ash. When he began to speak everyone listened!

"When I bowl a bouncer," he began slowly – we exchanged incredulous looks – "I try to kill the batsman." Poor Ken, we never let him forget it, and the more he tried the further we had to walk to fetch the ball!

Of course, one immediate effect of an organised Christian presence in university sport was that Christianity became an issue for discussion. When I first played for the university I don't remember a single conversation about Christ ever taking place. Now Christianity became a major topic of conversation.

I was helped by being adopted as a *cause célèbre* by cricket writer, Alan Gibson, of *The Times*. The fact that I was an aspiring clergyman and destined, in his view, to lead my team to the *Church Times* Cup final as Rural Dean of Dorchester, was, apparently, of great interest to this former Methodist lay preacher.

In 1975 when I nicked my way to 50 against Sussex, Gibson offered a small bet through his column in *The Times* that I would make a half-century at Lord's against Cambridge. My brother-in-law, never averse to a winning opportunity, and aware, after hours of bowling at me in the garden, that such a thing was unlikely, took him on. A week or two later a report appeared in *The Times* to the effect that during an innings of 6 against Gloucestershire Wingfield Digby had hooked the formidable South African fast bowler, Michael Proctor, for 4. Gibson continued, "the friends and relatives of Wingfield Digby will be relieved to hear that he was bowling off-breaks at the time."

Anyway, the existence of the Christians in Sport group and the attentions of Alan Gibson gave me a certain notoriety which I was careful to exploit. Others did, too. We played Derbyshire, captained by Eddie Barlow, that marvellous South African all-rounder. Quite a crowd assembled in the Parks to watch the great man. I had the honour of bowling the first ball to him. It was short of a length, lifted, hit his glove and dollied to gulley for an easy catch. After the close of play I was modestly talking the boys through this achievement while relaxing in a shower. My reverie was interrupted by the unmistakable face of Barlow peering round the wall of the shower. "Where's that *!*! vicar," he shouted, "I'm going to kill him!"

On another occasion we were playing Leicestershire. Their wicket-keeper was Roger Tolchard. As usual I got out cheaply – that was normal at Oxford, sometimes twice in one day! I confess that in those days a mild, but definitely unchristian oath passed my lips whenever I got out. In the pavilion at tea-time Roger came up to me, "I thought you were going to be a vicar," he said smiling, but semi-serious. "Vicars aren't meant to use language like that."

I was very ashamed of myself. It is only when I drop a catch that I am really tested now!

A more bizarre incident occurred against Glamorgan on the day before the Queen's Jubilee in 1977. Glamorgan's opening bowler was a West Indian Welshman called Tony Cordle. He was bowling us out on a damp morning. The score was about 60 for 6 when I came in and the batsman at the other end kept playing and missing. As he walked past me at the non-striker's end, Tony said, "I want to go to church tomorrow."

Now that is an unusual opening gambit during a first-class cricket match. Before I had a chance to reply he had gone to the end of his run-up. Next ball, the same thing happened. We were getting nowhere. I feared that the batsman facing would score a single, I would have strike and would probably get out straight away. Tony might not be so keen to talk about church with his team-mates around. It was now or never.

So, next ball I walked back with him to the end of his run-up arranging a rendezvous next morning. After all, I was an ambassador for Christ and here was a clear opportunity! Unfortunately, my action put me in a dilemma. I was with Tony 25 yards behind the umpire. I expect it is the only time in first-class cricket that the batsman and bowler have run in together, parting as they got to the umpire!

Tony failed to turn up for church.

By no means all of us who attended those early Christians in Sport meetings in Oxford were Christians. Some were antagonistic, some searching, others committed. But we found it congenial to discuss spiritual things in the context of sport. Others in different parts of the country were finding the same thing and before too long an opportunity came my way which was to have a great effect on Sue and myself.

Orlando

To my utter amazement Eddie Waxer invited us to join a group of ten people from England whom he wanted to attend a sports conference in Orlando, Florida. It was February 1977. February is always a bleak month for me (perhaps it stems from those hockey afternoons at school). But February in an Anglican theological college is as John McEnroe would say the "pits" – cold, damp, depressing. To be asked to spend eight days in a sun-soaked paradise – free – was quite a proposal. The college released me. With our friend, triple university blue, Helen Bayley, we travelled to Heathrow to meet our companions.

It is worth recording this in some detail. Again and again in the development of sports ministry we have found that progress is made, encouragement transmitted and faith strengthened when sportsmen and sportswomen who are Christians meet one another. Most Christians in sport are the only believers in their team. They are spiritually isolated and quickly discouraged. By this time I had met only a few Christians involved in sport and all in the university context.

At the airport we were introduced to our travelling companions. Mike Pusey was then pastor of the Farnborough Baptist Church. He was chaplain to Aldershot FC. He had made a link with the club on his own initiative and was keen to explore the American sports ministry. John Kilford at that time was a curate in Tonbridge. John had played professional football with Leeds and Notts County, but had great reservations about getting involved in football again. Peter Warfield was at Cambridge University and had won a cap or two as the centre for the England rugby team. His career was prematurely ended by injury a year or so later. Harry Hughes, a man everyone warms to instantly, was there. Gerald Williams was at least a familiar voice. His BBC Radio 2 tennis commentaries were well known.

The party was completed by the Rev. Alan Godson. Before Heathrow we had never met. First encounters with "Godders" can be unnerving. Kevin Simms – England centre three-quarter – recounts how he was in the changing-room after a northern division match against Romania in 1984, enjoying a celebratory drink and a singsong after a famous victory. The festivities were interrupted by the arrival of a solidly-built balding man. Kevin was standing between the two second-row forwards when Alan presented him with a booklet entitled something like, "Live every moment with Jesus". Kevin alternately wanted to die or kill Godson – probably both and in reverse order. Great enjoyment was had by all at Kevin's expense. A year later, though, at a men's dinner in Newmarket, Kevin testified to the importance of that afternoon as everyone in the team knew he was a Christian from then on . . . he could be a secret disciple no longer.

Alan is the kind of man who puts you on the spot . . . usually it is very uncomfortable. Later you are grateful. Alan knows the truth and he speaks the truth, but it sometimes takes people a while to realise it. Alan himself says that he is always aware that God is sharing His truth with everyone already. The signs of God can be seen around us in nature, in other people and of course in the Bible. Alan sees himself as coming in on the appropriate wavelength – tuning in to how the Spirit of God is already communicating with people.

For most of us the flight to Florida was an adventure. For Godson it was five and a half hours with a captive audience. I expect we were a great disappointment to him. He got into a long conversation with a stewardess – a very pretty stewardess! On the way home, to no one's surprise, because these things happen with Alan all the time, the same stewardess was looking after us. According to Alan she confessed Christ over Land's End!

On another trip home from the US – four years later – I was sitting next to Alan, reading my book. He got into conversation with a woman across the aisle. Her husband was asleep beside her. Occasionally, Godson would whisper to me, "pray", or "she's nearly through" . . . and eventually he prayed with her and she came to Christ. In due course, in fact as we landed, her husband awoke. There was no time for Alan to talk to him, but I noticed as we collected our bags that he was looking very suspiciously at us as his wife pointed us out.

"He looks a bit hostile," I remarked.

"Not surprising, is it?" says Alan. "He's discovering he's got a new wife!" Alan's interventions are not machine-like or artificial. Talking about Jesus and challenging people to think about their lives before God is as natural to him as breathing. He feels, to put it bluntly, "constrained by the love of Christ" to speak out.

Once in Miami we were billeted with friends of Eddie

Waxer for a couple of nights before the onward flight to
Orlando for the annual conference of the Pro Athletes
Outreach. While in Miami we attended a patriotic-cum-
Christian evening at the Key Biscayne Presbyterian
Church. The pastor, Steve Brown, in a somewhat un-
characteristic display of hyperbole welcomed the ten
people "who are going to change the world". We all
looked round wondering who could possibly be there.
"They've come from London, England," continued
Steve, and we took a rather embarrassed bow.

Eddie had done his work well on Steve and on us. As
Gerald Williams says, "Eddie had faith that Great Britain
would in time be the most significant country in the
world for the sending of athletes who know Christ to
other nations." When in October 1985 with the first
Christians in Sport cricket team we met Eddie in Bangalore, South India, I reminded him of that early vision and
we rejoiced in the power of prayer and God's faithful-
ness.

Orlando is the home of Disney World – a playground
for the rich and beautiful – a place where everyone can be
a "kid" again for a while. But for us, Orlando was the
location for a conference of about 150 professional
sportsmen and their wives. Mostly they were giant
American footballers with household names, big cars,
glamorous wives and, above all else, Jesus. They had
come, at their own expense, to learn how to share their
Christian faith more effectively.

The ten of us will have different memories. For Sue and
myself, we were won over by the love of the people and
their enthusiasm for the Gospel. It was infectious and we
felt very close as a couple that week.

On the last day of the conference there was an
opportunity for people to share what they had learnt
during the past few days. One large white man grabbed
the microphone like a striking rattlesnake. He had been
brought up in the South. Whites and blacks kept their
distance. Even in the locker-room the whites changed in

one part and the blacks in another. They drank and
socialised separately. They were different. He assumed it
and respected it. He had been horrified to discover that
there were blacks in his "huddle" (Bible-study group) on
the conference. For a couple of days he had kept quiet,
resentful, but he wanted to say now that he had been
wrong all those years. He loved those brothers and he
wanted them to know it.

It was very emotional in the hall, by now, silent, the
way it can be when a speaker is tugging at the heart-
strings. The silence was broken by a great crash at the
back of the room as one of the black men brought his fist
down on the table. Leaping to his feet, he shouted
"Hal-le-lu-jah!" at the top of his voice. They were
brothers in Christ and they had just discovered it.

We returned to London determined to do all we could
to build a Christian presence in sport in Great Britain. We
could see the enormous need for sportspeople to be
presented with the challenge of Jesus and we could see
more clearly than before that the impact of the testimony
in word and deed of Christian athletes is great indeed.

3

The Delivery Stride

Gerald Williams

For one man, Gerald Williams, that trip to Orlando was especially significant. He writes in *A Whole New Ball Game*:

> Towards the end of the week something was rankling me. Most of the sportsmen there talked freely of the day when they had "given their lives to the Lord", but I could not do that. I considered myself a Christian. What else had my christening and confirmation been about? I had become a sidesman at our local parish church at home.
>
> However, if there was something I had to do to be absolutely certain, some positive act to resolve my confusion, I was prepared to make that final request. One evening before we left Orlando, two or three of us knelt in my room, and, hesitantly, I asked Jesus to enter my life, so that I could be certain that it happened there, that day . . . it had been a disturbing, encouraging week. Deep feelings had been touched, and some cherished traditions questioned. We climbed into our Jumbo feeling that God could do something through Christians in Sport in Britain, if we made ourselves available.

To get inside Gerald Williams you need to know that he is a journalist. People who have been trained to sniff out stories never lose that ability.

Gerald is greatly respected in tennis – he's a BBC tennis correspondent – because he reports on tennis. He knows many details of the players' lives, indeed, as a Christian acts often in a counselling role, but all the players know that he would never use such confidences against them.

Gerald, you must realise, is also a Welshman. There is a fervour about him which is a characteristic of that nation. A Welsh friend of mine told me how his mother ripped his shirt from his back in excitement one afternoon at Cardiff Arms Park when Wales were playing England at rugby. Neither mother nor son noticed until the final whistle!

But most of all you need to know that Gerald is a Christian. He is a passionate follower of Jesus. Christianity was ingrained in him, but not until Orlando did he meet the risen Christ and begin to experience the power of the Holy Spirit in his life. Since then there have been great changes in his life. He had been married twice and both had ended in divorce accompanied by inevitable heartache and suffering. These wounds left their mark. His growing faith has helped him come to terms with these disappointments. Through the ministry of the Ewell Fellowship and Millmead Baptist Church in Guildford he became more and more convinced in the truth of what he believed and the reality of his experience of Jesus.

Many people told him that if he wanted to get on in his career, he must keep religion out of his broadcasts. But Gerald was not prepared for that. He knew the truth of the adage – "If Jesus Christ be Lord at all, He must be Lord of all." He has been unashamedly Christian in his job and broadcasts. Far from being ushered into the background, his career has taken off. The familiar voice has become a familiar face. His Wimbledon highlights programme which he co-hosts with his close friend Desmond Lynam is compulsive viewing for tennis buffs. He has even received the ultimate accolade – one of the "Sunday Awfuls'" vote for "Wally of the Week". The fish symbol he wears in his lapel proclaims his first allegiance to millions of viewers – he is Christ's man, and for many, including myself, a trusted friend.

On our return to England in February 1977, we found that what God was doing in Gerald's life, He was doing in many others, too. Our first faltering steps had been taken before and during the Orlando conference. But now we were entering the delivery stride, and it was God who was at work.

Bear in mind that in 1974/5 Eddie Waxer had found it difficult to find any committed Christian people in British sport. During the next few years, often quite independently of any organised activities, the situation altered quite radically. I should like to introduce you to a few of the people who would openly call themselves Christians, and regard their commitment to Christ as the most important thing in their lives.

Alan Knott

I was sitting in Alan and Jan Knott's dining-room in their Herne Bay home. We had met only once before, when Kent played the Combined Universities in the Benson and Hedges tournament a few years before. I had heard that Alan and Jan were Christians and had invited myself to lunch.

This was a terrific thrill for me. Alan is one of the greatest wicket-keeper batsmen in the history of cricket. His acrobatic wicket-keeping and idiosyncratic batting style had been familiar features of the England team for the last fifteen years. His continual stretching exercises and peculiar idiosyncracies – handkerchief half out of the pocket and touching the bails before batting – were known to all cricket lovers. He was simply "Knottie" – a great player.

"You give thanks, Andrew," he said in his voice which I have only heard Graham Cowdrey, another Christian cricketer, successfully imitate.

"Oh, people always ask a vicar," I replied. "You give thanks."

"Hello Jesus," prays Alan, "just a word to say thanks before we get stuck in."

Now people don't normally pray like that. We shut our eyes, bow our heads, look religious and say things like, "Dear Lord, Heavenly Father . . ." but that is not Knottie's way. As he says in his autobiography *It's Knott Cricket* (Macmillan), Jesus is his "greatest friend". He's with him all the time, he can talk to Him all the time. You don't need a church building or religious language because in its simplest and truest form, being a Christian is having a relationship, a friendship with God.

Alan was not brought up in an overtly Christian way, but he began to pray at an early age. The words "through Jesus Christ, our Lord" brought him freedom from nightmares and fears. In the early 1970s he met some American Christians who shared their faith with him and his wife, but it was at a service at the Kensington Temple in London that Alan and Jan eventually accepted the invitation to commit their lives to Christ.

Alan is an intensely private man, almost fastidious, organising his time very carefully. Christian people asking him to share his faith at their churches invaded that privacy and he was very put off the organised Church. But his friendship with Jesus flourished over the years and Alan has become renowned throughout the world of cricket as a man of integrity and solid Christian commitment.

At Lord's one day, he introduced me to the Kent captain, Asif Iqbal, a Pakistani and a real gentleman. "You're a religious man, Asif," said Alan. "Meet Andrew, he's a vicar."

"I am religious," replied the Moslem Asif, "but if I was half as good a man as Alan, I would be happy."

Of course, we must always avoid equating "goodness" with being a Christian. Christians should try to be good, or at least better than they were, but "being good" does not make you a Christian.

Alan is never ashamed of speaking up for Jesus, and he longs for his fellow professionals to hear about Jesus and welcome Him into their lives.

At Worcester towards the end of the 1985 season, I was in the Kent dressing-room at tea-time.

"Hey, ——," Knottie called to one of the players, "you've got a problem with pornography; you'd better have a word with Andrew, here!"

I'm not sure who was more embarrassed, myself or the player concerned, especially when he found out I was a clergyman.

Over the years Alan has got more involved in Christians in Sport, but he remains a private, family man. His concern is to develop his friendship with the Lord and be the kind of person in his business and personal life that his "friend" wants him to be. He's not a preacher, and there's no reason why he should be. The quality of his life is eloquent to the truth that a relationship with Christ is sufficient to fulfil anybody.

Alan West

Alan and Cathy West grew up in the north-west of England with no religious influence at all. Alan became a professional footballer as a lad and after serving his apprenticeship at Burnley (where he rubbed shoulders with Joe Brown) he was transferred to Luton Town, where he played throughout the 1970s. Eventually he left Luton and played for a couple of seasons at Millwall, before retiring from league football and concentrating on being player-manager of non-league Hitchin Town and training for the Christian ministry.

How the rough, hard-swearing lager-loving boy from Burnley became the gentle, caring, whole man of God that he is today is a fascinating story.

Two apparently unrelated events were used by God to bring Alan and Cathy to Christ. First of all there was a boom in American soccer during the 1970s. Alan spent a few seasons in the US playing with the Minnesota Kicks. They loved America. The hype, the style, the friendliness of the Americans bowled them over.

Second, a few years earlier Cathy's parents had emigrated to New Zealand. So in 1976 Alan and Cathy decided to fly on from America to visit them. Now Cathy's parents' marriage had been very rocky when they left and the move was a pretty desperate attempt to salvage their relationship. The Wests were somewhat apprehensive when they arrived – it could be a tricky visit.

What they discovered astonished them. Cathy's parents told them that they had joined a church (a church!) and become Christians. Of course, Alan and Cathy didn't know what they were on about. But over the next three weeks they met other members of the church and attended services with Cathy's parents. Their marriage was working again. They had found a new purpose and peace in life which set the Wests thinking.

Alan takes up the story. "What we noticed was that these people, whether they were rich or poor, had a quality of life that was certainly not part of our lives at that time. They explained that Jesus had died so we could be forgiven and that He was alive and that it was He who gave this new life." Of course, there was great heart-searching, but before they left New Zealand, Alan and Cathy knelt down together and asked the Lord to come into their lives.

Alan's team-mates must have wondered what on earth had happened when a very different Westie reported for training. Alan and Cathy had been converted overnight. They were instantly very different. Of course, there was much to learn and much to change, but the difference was immediately apparent. Alan didn't swear any more, he drank less, church and the weekly fellowship group were priorities in their diaries. Alan began to share his new faith with his team-mates and at local youth clubs and men's meetings.

Initially he had been apprehensive about talking about Jesus at the club. Sport is a pretty ruthless war zone and anything that singles you out is easily exploited. But Alan found that as he tried to live his Christian life he earned the respect of his colleagues and many would ask him questions. He also found that they trusted him more, and would share personal things in their lives with him – worries about transfers, contracts, loss of form and even marriage problems.

He also found that his commitment to football increased. He had always loved playing (unlike some pros) and had been a hard trainer. But, in his opinion at least, he now worked even harder at his game. He knew now that his great talent was a gift from God and that in using it he was playing not only for himself and the team, but for God.

Alan's conversion caused considerable media interest and he was interviewed on radio and by newspaper reporters about his faith. Because Alan is a straightforward, palpably honest man he received sympathetic treatment.

The crowds were not always so sympathetic, however. If the team were losing, cries of "Start praying, Westie!" would drift across the ground at Kenilworth Road. If he was having a bad game they would shout, "Read your Bible, Westie!" Once he knelt down to do up his laces before taking a throw-in – "Saying your prayers, are you lad?" came a shout from behind him. Most of this was done in fun, but sometimes it hurt. It's not easy being a Christian anywhere these days, but it can be very hard in the rough-and-tumble world of professional sport.

Richie Powling

Another footballer who became a Christian around this time was Richie Powling. He was a constructive (he

would say destructive!) midfield player for Arsenal and
the England under-21 side. I didn't know Richie before
he was a Christian, but I've talked about him with Ian
Gould, later to be a Middlesex, Sussex and England
cricketer, who was a fellow apprentice "gunner" with
Richie. They were great mates in those days – a couple of
rough Cockney diamonds, pure, natural, untreated
gems. I bumped into Gouldie at Lord's one day:

"Saw a friend of yours last night, Gouldie."

"Who was that then, Wingers old son?"

"Richie Powling – he's become a Christian, you
know," I replied.

"What? Come off it, mate – not Rich. Give us a break!"

I don't know what they got up to as teenagers in
Highbury, but clearly it had precious little to do with
Bible studies and church meetings!

It all began during Richie's engagement to a lovely
blonde PE teacher called Elaine, who is now his wife.
They were to be married in three weeks, and had bought
a home in Ilford. Some friends invited them to hear a talk
by a local evangelist, Trevor Dearing.

Most would agree that by any estimation Trevor was,
and probably still is, a bit of a wild man when it comes to
preaching the Gospel. No holds are barred, and decisions are called for and expected.

The message really was news to Richie and he sat
amazed and thrilled at what he was hearing. It was as if
the words were meant just for him. At the close of his
address Trevor asked anyone who was ready to invite
Jesus into their lives as Lord and Saviour, to indicate by
raising a hand.

"Nothing was going to get me to raise my hand," said
Richie later. "But I looked up and my hand was in the
air!"

Trevor then invited all those who had done this to
come forward and be prayed for publicly that they might
enter into a "full experience of God".

"Nothing was going to get me out of my seat and make

me walk forward," says Richie, "but then I found myself kneeling at the front and being prayed for and knowing that Jesus was in my life."

Together Richie and Elaine left that meeting knowing he was different and that life would never be the same again. He walked around the streets feeling as if he were going to explode, more thrilled and elated than he had ever been when scoring goals at Highbury.

Elaine was troubled. She had felt nothing and been convinced of nothing. She felt that it had all been very emotional and "her man", to whom she was to be married in three weeks, had been swept away from her.

"He was completely different," she says, "and I couldn't reach that part of him at all."

In this condition they got married and a difficult time it was for them both. Richie knew he had found "gold"; Elaine thought she had married a religious maniac. Fortunately they joined a sensible, caring, local church and in due course, over a year later, Elaine committed her life to Christ.

No sooner had Richie been converted and married than he sustained a bad knee injury. Three years of struggle against this injury began; there were operations, and more operations. Each time it seemed hopeful, but he always broke down again, playing for the reserves.

They tried prayers for healing, but even those had no effect. After three years he was forced out of the game.

What was happening to the Powlings was the nightmare from which no professional sportsman or sportswoman is exempt. They all know that injury can end their careers just like that. Of course, there are insurance policies which in theory can at least protect them from financial ruin . . . yet it's surprising how many get caught out by the small print.

Sadly, many sportspeople have their self-respect, their identity wrapped up in their sports achievement. When the ability to perform is denied, then a crisis can follow. Some turn disastrously to drink or drugs. On December

29th, 1985, the *Sunday Times* carried an article entitled, "The giddy fall from Highbury to heroin". A contemporary of Richie's – whom I shall not name, though the *Sunday Times* did – had suffered a similar injury. "Drug dependency set in almost as quickly as arthritis. An old friend offered heroin to ease 'X's' withdrawal pangs and he became hooked . . . heroin wrecked his marriage . . . he was stabbed three times as he got out of his car in South London." Others immerse themselves in gambling which inevitably leads to financial ruin.

Every professional sports club has its individuals whose lives have been wrecked by injury and the resulting failure to cope.

So how would Richie and Elaine cope with this trauma? The first thing to say is that it has been difficult. They have a young family and Richie has continually been frustrated at his attempts to play even non-league football. There have been bleak periods and hard times. The Christian is not immune from the problems everyone else faces.

But Richie and Elaine knew that their identity, their self-respect, depended not on their achievements but on Christ. Whether you win or lose, He cares for you; whether you are fit or injured, Christ has a purpose for you. So they have survived, indeed they have done more than that, they have grown as people and in their faith.

At that rather emotional meeting in Romford Richie laid hold of life for the first time. When all that he had previously valued was snatched away from him and his family, he discovered that we need nothing except Jesus.

Overseas

As Christian sportspeople have emerged in our own country so it has been throughout the world.

In the autumn of 1977 I was ordained and we moved to serve in the Anglican church at Cockfosters in North

London. We found that the basis for a Christians in Sport
group in the area existed. Harry Hughes was, by now,
firmly ensconced at Spurs just down the road. Watford
Football Club had appointed a local Baptist minister,
John Boyers, as their chaplain. Alan West was playing for
Luton Town and Richie Powling was still at Arsenal. BBC
football commentator, John Motson, lived in St Albans
and was already an open supporter of Christians in
Sport.

So, although Sue and I were busy in our new life, our
involvement with the growing sports ministry increased.

In the summer of 1978 we made our second visit to the
States. Christ Church, Cockfosters, which remains
firmly supportive of the work, helped us with the air
fares. Once in New York we travelled on the Greyhound
buses like thousands of other tourists.

Eddie Waxer had set up a tour of the North-East which
would expose us to different aspects of the Christian
presence in sport in his country. The overall impression
we gained was that at every level of sport it is not at all
unusual to find deeply-committed Christians.

For instance, every one of the professional American
football teams had a chaplain who ran a chapel service
before each game. Sometimes members of both teams
would attend. Sue and I could not help but be amused at
the thought of these huge men praying together before
going out and engaging each other in what seemed to us
ferociously violent combat.

One morning in Cleveland, Ohio, we arranged to have
breakfast in a downtown hotel with the chaplain of the
Cleveland Browns, Bob Provost. The meeting was uneventful except for the fact that we could not get out of the
hotel for some reason. We found ourselves trapped in a
passageway outside the kitchens with a pile of what
Americans call "trash cans". The only way out was by
climbing over them, which we duly did. The church
where Bob was then ministering – the Chapel in the Park
at Akron – generously supported our work in the early

days and in our correspondence we often reminisce on this rather unpromising start to our relationship. It gave a whole new slant to St Paul's words to the Philippians in the New Testament, "I count all things rubbish, that I may gain Christ"(3:8).

At Michigan State University we attended a conference of the Fellowship of Christian Athletes. This turned out to be a real eye-opener. In Britain it is still unusual to be keen on Christianity and sport. In school Christian groups there is often an absence of really sporty pupils. It is the same at universities and colleges – the Christian unions give the impression of being most popular with the earnest, scholarly, guitar-strumming physicist rather than the party-loving rugby full back. Certainly one of the main functions of the Christians in Sport university groups has been to provide a congenial atmosphere in which sportsmen and sportswomen can consider Jesus.

At Michigan we were surrounded by athletes, fresh-faced all-American "kids" whose enthusiasm for sports was outdone only by their enthusiasm for Jesus. Sue joined a "wives' huddle", expecting coffee-drinking Bible studies, and found herself engaged in an exhausting merry-go-round of volley-ball, tennis, racket-ball and, "Gee, Sue, how about a neat game of squash?"

It's a funny thing with Americans, when you anticipate seeing them, or look back on your time with them, you think in your very British way that they are quite outrageous, embarrassing and totally over the top. But when you are with them, it's great.

Of course, they said, "We just love your accent." I kept telling them that they had accents, not us, but they were unconvinced.

What we discovered during the three weeks we travelled around was that born-again Christian sportspeople have had a great impact on the people of North America. Many of those with whom we stayed identified politicians, movie stars and athletes as the most influential groups. The moral standards and religious views adopted by these groups were undoubtedly studied and adopted by many others in society. They have even made a movie star President!

We could not help but feel that many of the role models presented to our young people in Britain by these groups were anything but Christian. Again we returned to England very aware of the need for a Christian presence in sport.

Over the next couple of years I was invited to conferences in Washington and Hong Kong and began to meet some of the other people involved in sports ministries and some of the stars who had become Christians.

Larry Nelson

The 1983 American PGA tournament was played at Atlanta, Georgia. A local boy who had not taken up golf until he was twenty-one was four shots clear going into the last round. The "boy" was Larry Nelson and he suggested to his wife, Gayle, that they should go to their local church as his tee-time was not until 3 p.m.

It was not unusual that the Nelsons should all go to church. They are all deeply committed Christians and one of the leading couples on the Christian golf scene. But it was certainly uncommon for the leader of one of the major tournaments of the year to spurn practice in favour of church on the morning of the biggest round of golf in his life. Larry had never won a "major" before.

He was, not unnaturally, very nervous as he walked into church that day and hoped that something in the service, perhaps a hymn or a word from the preacher would calm his nerves. As so many do when they get to church, he looked through the hymns that were due to be sung, hoping as we all do, that they will be familiar. But he was also looking for that "word".

His eye wandered through the words of the first hymn

until arrested by the sentence ". . . and they shall all lay down their trophies".

"Oh no," he thought, "that's not what I need at all." He moved on to the next song and was relieved to discover it began "Victory in Jesus". He praised the Lord, listened to the sermon, and went out and won the PGA title.

Speaking at the Wentworth Golf Club the day after Nick Faldo won the British Open at Muirfield in 1987, Larry explained that singing that chorus had helped him. Everything in his life depended on Jesus's victory and not on his success or failure in the golf tournament. Those victories will pass away, but not Christ's. He said how much he would love to see his own name on the British Open trophy; but he continued, "I won't see my name there for long – it'll have to give others pleasure, because I will be dead and gone."

Winning that title gave Larry exemption from qualifying for the British Open and it was at Troon in 1983 that he got involved with Christians in Sport. We arranged for him to come and conduct a golf clinic and speak at a dinner in Hadley Wood Golf Club. (By this time I was minister at St Paul's, a little church in the trees, in that delightful North London suburb.) It was the enlightened policy of the golf club to grant honorary membership to the local clergyman, a perk I enjoyed enormously but which was insufficient to improve my golf very much.

Larry had finished well up the field in the Open and so was warmly received by the golfers at the club. What impressed them, apart from his golf swing, was his charm and ease of manner. He had come straight from the most important championship in the world; he must have been tired and looking forward to rejoining his family in Atlanta. Yet nothing was too much trouble. He made a point of meeting the club pro and seeing his shop. He introduced himself to the members next to whom he changed in the locker-room. He commended

Christ in his whole manner, and even the hardest-nosed
businessman was touched by his sincerity and warmth.

Hadley Wood Golf Club is one of those that protects its
standards. There are strict dress rules. Unfortunately, in
true American style, Larry did not have the statutory
jacket and tie . . . in his case the rule was waived, but it
was with undisguised delight that the club captain
presented him with the club tie at the end of his speech.

Washington

In the autumn of 1979 four of us from England were
invited to attend a sports ministers' conference in
Washington DC. I was accompanied by Alan Godson (by
now chairman of Christians in Sport), John Boyers, who
was also the minister of St James Rd Baptist Church,
Watford, just around the corner from the Vicarage Road
ground, and Dave Merrington, that hard-tackling defender who had been introduced to the Christian faith by
Joe Brown at Burnley.

Dave had just been sacked as assistant manager at
Leeds United and was very unsure about his future in the
game. After three very troubled years, he in fact returned
to football, moved south and became youth team coach at
Southampton. In 1979, though, his future was very
uncertain.

A classic example of the problems of ministering to
professional footballers is provided by an attempt to get
Dave to Heathrow Airport on time. It is important to
realise that since the age of sixteen most top soccer
players have had just about everything done for them.
They are often housed, fed, transported, clothed and
generally supervised. Furthermore, I suspect, though I
don't know, the coaching they are given encourages
them to fit into a team pattern in the squad. Individual
expression is unfashionable in British sport, or at least
there is precious little of it!

Anyway, we four had been invited to Washington. The tickets were provided for us, but we did have to apply for and collect the necessary visas from the American Embassy. Unfortunately, Dave arrived in London on the morning of the flight without a visa. He also had a grave suspicion of London taxis, but I did manage to persuade him that Washington DC would remain only a dream unless we started using one!

Anyway, we did make it to the plane in time, but I was asking myself, "Who would manage a football team for a living?"

One afternoon in Washington we decided to do some sightseeing together. I'm a hopeless sightseer, but a considerable fan of American history and especially Abraham Lincoln – so, all I wanted to do was wander along to the Lincoln Memorial and read the Gettysburg address which is inscribed on the wall of what is a stunning place.

But not Dave – he had to see the lot. We jogged round the White House perimeter fence, bunny-hopped over the lawns in front of the Washington monument (I can't tell you what he said about that!), sprinted round the space museum and finally collapsed on the steps of the Lincoln Memorial. Cheers, Dave! I don't think I have been sightseeing since!

Apart from the rigours of spending ten days with Merrington, Washington was another rung in the ladder leading me to full-time work in sports, and further encouragement to Christians in Sport. We met people there from many different countries.

Brian Booth

From Australia came Test cricketer Brian Booth. Brian batted in the Australian middle order when I was at my most impressionable age. How I hated Lawry, Simpson, Harvey, O'Neill, Burge, Booth, Mackay, Benaud, Grout,

Davidson, and MacKenzie! These were the bogy men of my early teens and their names are etched in my memory. But there were some great players in that side and Brian Booth was a key figure.

In Washington Boothie was my room-mate. He was feeling off-colour when he left Sydney and had deteriorated on the flight. An American doctor diagnosed stones in the kidney and put him on a high fluid intake – no sacrifice for an Aussie, you might think! Anyway, it looked as if he would miss some of the best sessions of the conference. Alan Godson happened to be in our room and was sitting on the floor while Brian was telling me how rough he felt.

"We've got to pray about this," said Alan. So, kneeling in front of Brian with his hands on his knees, Alan prayed simply and unemotionally for Brian to be made well. Alan has a sportsman's down-to-earth relationship with God, so he simply told the Lord that there was no point in bringing Boothie all the way from Sydney to Washington if he was going to be lying sick in bed!

At the end of the prayer I could see that Brian was deeply moved, almost in tears. Later, I asked Brian why he had been so touched by Alan's prayer – it had seemed unremarkable to me.

Brian replied, "I have been prayed for many times in public. As a Test cricketer I was always getting prayed for, but no one has ever knelt like that in front of me and prayed so caringly." He quickly recovered and missed none of the conference sessions.

It was Brian who encouraged me in my dream of taking a Christian cricket team to India. I had thought about it before, but Brian had played there and he told me about the huge crowds and the idolisation of the cricketers. What a platform Christian players would have to share their faith!

Sadly, Brian's commitments in Australia were to prevent his returning to India when the tour eventually took place. His stories both alarmed and excited me.

During the second Test of the tour in Bombay the Australians were accommodated actually in the Brabourne Stadium where the match was played. Brian remembers Indian fans wandering into the players' bedrooms to get autographs.

RANGOON
RUNS.

Things deteriorated even more in Calcutta where the third Test was played. Brian was suffering particularly badly from that well-known disease on the subcontinent, "Delhi Belly". He takes up the story.

It was not a high-scoring match – at the end of the first day we were 6 for 167. I was lying on the couch "crook", afflicted by gripey pains. The dressing-room under the stand was noisy. Lawry and Simpson put on 97 for the frist wicket before 3 wickets fell quickly. Remember I was "crook". I was out first ball bowled by Durani, a left-hand spinner. The ball turned from feet outside leg stump to off. I hit it full in the middle of the bat, but when it hit the pitch it spun viciously back on to my stumps. I went back to the changing-room and climbed back on to the couch, where I remained for some time!

I bet he did.

Brian Booth was a Christian throughout his playing days and earned the respect of fellow players and fans for his consistent witness to Jesus Christ.

There was a large contingent from South America in Washington. They all impressed us with their commitment to Christ and also by their determination to reach their footballers with the Gospel. In recent years they have succeeded in this aim and there are numerous committed Christians playing in top South American football.

The leading figure in the Brazilian sports ministry is Alex Ribiero – the former racing driver whose "Jesus Saves" racing team attracted a lot of publicity at the end of the 1970s.

It was my first experience of praying with people who had no English. They would babble on in Spanish (I assume) with an occasional "Amen" or "Hallelujah", which we could all understand. And yet it really didn't matter at all that we didn't understand what they were saying. It seems strange, but we all sensed a deep unity and we knew we should agree with each other's prayers. We all knew we could say "Amen", though we had no understanding. Perhaps this is the language of heaven.

Hong Kong

In 1981 an even more ambitious conference with people involved in sports ministry from all around the world was held in Hong Kong. Whereas there were about thirty of us in Washington, there were 250 or so in Hong Kong.

The conference was arranged to coincide with a tour of China by a team of American basketball players. For three weeks this team of huge, top, mostly black American "ball" players played and conducted clinics in China, which for thirty-five years had been closed to the Gospel. Missionaries were still banned, but the government was more open to the West and in particular to Western sports teams. Simply because they were great basketball players, the team had opportunities to meet and share the Gospel discreetly with thousands of basketball fans and influential officials.

Each day at the conference we met to learn from each other and receive Biblical teaching. I remember at one breakfast session our time of praise before a talk from Key Biscayne's Steve Brown was led by Eddie Waxer – a Hebrew Christian from the States, and another man who was a Baptist pastor from Nazareth, Israel. He happened also to be a Palestinian. It was particularly poignant because on that very day the Palestinian Liberation Organisation was being evacuated from Beirut. While Jews and Palestinians fought to the death in the Middle East, Christ united them in Hong Kong.

There was a large contingent from India at the conference. Many of the delegates were not involved in sport – offer an air ticket to an Indian and he will always accept! But one genuine athlete from Bangalore was the Rev. Robin Paul who will figure prominently in the next chapter of this book.

Robin was a 400-metre runner, had represented India and competed in the Asian Games. He has become the key man for the sports ministry in India, though, because it is such a vast country, others are taking initiatives, too.

Robin and I immediately established a warm friendship which has been cemented over the years with visits to each other's countries. He shared my excitement about taking a Christian cricket team to India and the Hong Kong trip will always for me be the birthplace of the Indian tour.

4

Playing Forward

Planning the tour

When we parted in 1981, Robin Paul and I agreed that we
should plan for autumn 1984 as the best time for a cricket
tour of India. That would give him plenty of time to make
the necessary contacts in cricket in India, and develop
them to the point where there would be a good chance
that the best players would turn out against us. He was
concerned, as I was, about the financing of such an
ambitious scheme. My job was to raise a side of sufficient
standard to justify the venture. As it turned out, we
didn't in fact go until October 1985.

At that time I hoped to persuade Alan Knott and Brian
Booth to return to the subcontinent where they had
suffered so badly. There were three New Zealand Test
players, Yuile, Murray and Pollard, whom I knew were
Christians. I hoped they would come out of retire-
ment. From England I had my sights set on Vic Marks
(Somerset), Roland Butcher (Middlesex), Roger Knight
(Surrey), Simon Sutcliffe (Warwickshire), John Barclay
(Sussex) and a battery of former Oxford and Cambridge
players whom I knew to be strong Christians and
competent cricketers.

Perhaps in the end the quality of our side – certainly in
respect of reputation, which counts for so much in India –
was a disappointment.

The eventual team was captained by Vic Marks and
rather grandly named the International Ambassadors XI.

Vic Marks

Vic is a farmer's son from Middle Chinnock in the wilds of Somerset. It is quite unimaginable that he could have come from anywhere else. He is a Somerset man through and through. There is a slowness, even a tiredness, which disguises an active mind, a shrewd assessment of what is going on. Vic has rural wisdom in his bones.

Local historians would describe Vic's family as the "salt of the earth" and they would be on the right track. It was a secure, God-fearing, respectable upbringing which led him eventually to Blundell's School and St John's College, Oxford, where, somewhat surprisingly, he was reading Greats. Even now he cannot hide his own surprise that he actually knows things about Greek and ancient history.

He was, of course, an outstanding sportsman at school (cricket, rugby and fives especially). His arrival at Oxford coincided with my return for my theology course. He had a reputation based on merit and I was an "old blue". The first match of the 1975 season was against Sussex, Vic's first-class début, and to my amazement I made 69 runs – my career-best score.

For a while at least we were equals, but it did not take the next ten years for Vic to realise it was a flash in the pan.

In 1976 and 1977 Vic captained the university cricket team. What a happy and devoted team we were – winning the Varsity match in 1976. Vic's leadership is not charismatic in style . . . more cuddly. He spoke rarely and contented himself with putting his feet up and fiddling with his already thinning hair. I've often wondered why he was such a good captain. Perhaps it was his own high standards of performance we respected . . . but that is never enough on its own. Perhaps it was because he inspired confidence, giving the impression of believing in his players' ability, despite massive evidence to the contrary. I recall being put on to bowl against Glamorgan batsman Alan Lewis Jones and being hit for 26 in my first over. Up strolled Vic – never one to rush – put his arm around my shoulders, giggled and muttered in his exaggerated Somerset accent, "Try another one, Diggers". Perhaps it was because he never criticised people behind their backs that we trusted him. Perhaps it was his own obvious vulnerability as a person which made him honest and real. Whatever the reason, he was the best captain I ever played under and I suspect the great majority of the team would agree.

During his four years at Oxford, Vic met and started going out with Anna Stewart. Like me, she had come face to face with full-blooded Christian commitment at the Mayflower Family Centre. Like me, deep in her heart she was and remains something of a rebel. Her faith was expressed in involvement with Christian music and drama groups. To her amazement she responded to the courtship of the Somerset charmer – a non-Christian cricketer, whose sole claim to musical accomplishment was late-night guitar strumming and attempts at "The Streets of London".

Like many people, Vic had great respect for the Church and Christianity, but had never personally confronted the central issue of whether or not it was all true. Now he found himself surrounded by people who believed passionately and he began to read the New Testament. Gradually he reached the place where he had to acknowledge Jesus as the truth and he invited Christ into his life.

One link in the chain that eventually brought Vic to Christian commitment was a supper party which Sue and I organised. Eddie Waxer was on one of his visits from Florida and we asked him to speak briefly after supper. The guests were the entire university cricket team, crammed into our tiny flat. Sue cooked a delicious meal and we had a few glasses of beer before I introduced Eddie to the team. I had anticipated a ten-minute talk –

stimulating, direct, challenging – and then back to the beer and plenty of chat.

For fifty-five minutes Eddie explained why Christianity had to be true. Sue and I were quietly dying in the corner of the room. As far as I remember the talk, Eddie gave three reasons for believing in Christianity: (1) the Virginity of Mary; (2) the birth of Jesus in Bethlehem; and (3) the fact that Jesus was Jewish. Now these are not generally regarded as the central issues of Christianity! We assumed that nobody would be at all convinced. To our surprise, Vic seemed to be – which may be a reflection on a public-school and Oxford education. Anyway, he asked to talk further with Eddie, who invited him to breakfast the next morning. Our flat was at least two miles from where Vic lived. Furthermore, as everybody who knows Vic well – from his wife to Ian Botham – will tell you, he simply does not function before 10 a.m. But at 7 a.m. the next morning the doorbell rang and there he was. I don't know what transpired exactly during that conversation, but I do know that from then on, Vic was ready to be known as a Christian.

To the outsider the life that followed Oxford must seem exciting and successful. Having established himself in the Somerset side, Vic developed his bowling to the point that he was an indispensable part of England's one-day attack. He went on three successive England tours – to Australia, New Zealand, Pakistan and India – and played in six Test Matches. Almost certainly he would have made England's 1987 World Cup squad, but Anna was expecting their second child and he made himself unavailable. Somerset had also awarded him a benefit – so he had plenty to do at home.

Things are, however, not always as good as they seem. Soon after leaving Oxford, Vic and Anna got married, and almost immediately Anna became pregnant and Amy arrived. Anna is a compelling, intelligent and vital woman. She did not find it all easy to be left at home with a baby while her husband travelled the country playing county cricket. She was frustrated by her inability to pursue her career in zoology and lonely without Vic. Somehow in the struggle to keep their lives and their marriage together, God seemed irrelevant. At no time did they stop believing, but it was a rough time.

But they had found a Bible-based church, St George's, Tiverton, and over the years they have made real Christian friends there, and God has again and again proved Himself faithful. For Vic and Anna, living the Christian life has often been hard; combining professional cricket and being a Christian has been a terrific challenge to Vic. He would be the first to admit his failures. Alan Knott was very amused when Vic uttered a mild oath at the crease. Immediately he turned round and said, "Oh, sorry, Knottie, forgot you were there!"

Like flowers, Christians have to grow. Some bloom almost immediately, and there is a danger of equally speedy withering. For Vic and Anna the growth has been unspectacular. But through the pain of their separations and the frustrations of Anna's career, they have put roots deep down into the love of God. To themselves, they often feel like failures; to the superspiritual Christian observer they may seem a disappointment, but to those of us who know them and love them, their integrity and faith are a continual inspiration.

When contemplating the tour it was quite inconceivable to me that anyone but Vic should be captain. I am afraid he knew this and was under a certain amount of pressure. Considering how much time he had spent away from home, it was very good of him to come . . . and good of Anna to release him!

Jack Bond

The team coach was Lancashire County Cricket Club manager, Jack Bond. Jack had played for Lancashire in their glory years in the late 1960s and early 1970s and established a reputation as both a fine player and a skilful captain. No one who saw it will ever forget the astonishing catch he made to win a Gillette Cup final. He also played for a year or two with Nottinghamshire before returning to Old Trafford as team manager. He brought his wife, Florence, with him on the tour and they proved to be an inspired selection.

In Madras we all attended a service of healing on the second Sunday of the tour – it was actually the only time we all went to church together. We had to get up at 3.30 the next morning to fly to Hyderabad. As we gathered in the hotel lobby it seemed very quiet. Jack had lost his voice.

"What's the problem?" I asked rather lamely.

"I was OK till I went to that healing service," croaked Jack in reply, to everyone's huge amusement.

Our manager was a long-time friend of mine, Nigel Freeman, a member of the national executive of Christians in Sport. Nigel has organisational gifts as long as you can get him awake. He certainly did a marvellous job for us, negotiating our way through Indian officialdom and liaising closely with Robin Paul. Nigel's wife, Rosemary, accompanied us, too. She has a beautiful singing voice and was popular with all the churches we attended. She and Florence both struggled with the somewhat primitive facilities we encountered occasionally. When we spent a night in a game reserve looking for tigers – or was it dodos (they seemed equally rare) – they almost reached the end of their tethers. But they never let on to the rest of the team, and it was great having them with us.

Martindale and Cowdrey

The batting had been strengthened during the summer by the emergence on the Christian cricket scene of two bright young stars. Duncan Martindale originally responded to an advertisement which we had placed in the *Cricketer*.

"Dear Sir," he wrote, "I am a professional cricketer trying to glorify God by the way I play . . . Yours sincerely, Duncan Martindale."

With my superstars withdrawing their availability like wisdom teeth, this was good news. During the summer of 1985 Duncan forced his way into the Nottinghamshire side, scoring a maiden century against Jack Bond's Lancashire attack. He's a quiet and thoughtful man, with an inner strength stemming from his firm Christian commitment. He is also a mighty good player, a touch player really, especially strong off his legs.

Graham Cowdrey is a very different kind of man and player. He also had emerged as a Christian and a county cricketer during the summer of 1985, getting into a strong Kent batting line-up and scoring 50 against the touring Australians. Graham is an altogether more volatile character than Duncan. He likes to, and can, hit the ball incredibly hard (he scored prolifically throughout the tour). He is an aggressive seam bowler (more of that later) and a brilliant fielder.

He has not followed a smooth path to Christian commitment. Great expectations (he is the third son of Colin Cowdrey – the famous England batsman and my childhood hero) and the breakup of his parents' marriage when he was thirteen left him insecure and troubled throughout his teens. He felt "managed" as a cricketer, and immersed himself and his whole identity in a rock singer called Van Morrison. Still today if he's got his "Walkman" on you can be pretty sure he's tuned in to "Van the man".

At Durham University he met many Christians and attended the thriving St Nicholas's Church in the city centre from time to time. But it was in South Africa the following winter that the light began to dawn. Walking through Cape Town, his attention was grabbed by a church notice-board advertising a series of Lent addresses at lunch-times. He went in out of curiosity and returned each day. By the end of the week he was ready to make his first tentative step of Christian commitment.

Roger Knight

Roger Knight was a proven county player of great distinction. Sadly, he could join us for only a few days of the tour, and never got going with the bat. He is also, though, a "mean" one-day bowler and helped us there. Roger combines his firm and growing Christian faith with teaching.

The rest of the batting was supported by Jim Dewes – a Cambridge blue and son of a former Middlesex and England batsman; Phil Richardson, who was a student at Cambridge and also bowled off-breaks; Guy McDonnell, another Cambridge student, and Paul Moses of Tamil Nadu.

The bowling was strengthened by the late availability of Simon Hughes (Middlesex). "Yosser", as he is universally known, was on his way to Perth where he was spending the rest of the winter. Having struggled with injury during the 1985 season, he was glad of the opportunity for some bowling in not too demanding circumstances. Though from a Christian home, Simon would, I think, not have called himself a Christian, but he has an enquiring and open mind. He turned out to be a real asset on and off the field. Mark Frost was our second pace bowler. He is the son of a vicar, Durham University educated like Cowdrey and Hughes, and capable of an extraordinary dislocation of his shoulder-blade which enables him to do shark imitations in a swimming pool! Mark has gone on to play for Staffordshire, and at the time of writing is having trials with Surrey. John Knight (former Oxford University) was picked to bowl fast and did so on one occasion, but he turned out to be more of a batsman than a bowler. Simon Sutcliffe (Oxford University and a couple of years with Warwickshire) was a flighty off-spinner. He had been involved with the Oxford University Christians in Sport group and started a similar group at Loughborough where he trained to be a teacher.

Our wicket-keeper was Paul Fisher, my old friend from university days, and the party was completed by what Marks called "professional theologians". I certainly would make no such pretension, nor I think would Peter Swaffield (a cricketing Baptist minister then based at Upton Vale Church in Torquay) and Steve Wookey, a former colleague from Cockfosters, working in the Anglican Church in Paris. Steve had the distinction of winning blues both at Oxford and Cambridge as a fast bowler. He achieved some fame for getting Geoff Boycott out for 0. When Boycott was asked what he thought of Steve's bowling, he said, "Who the !*!* is Wookey?" When Steve was interviewed he said he thought that the caught and bowled might have been a bump ball. That may be taking modesty too far! We three were to take the brunt of the preaching while the others made runs and took wickets.

All this was a long way away when in the mid-summer of 1984 Robin Paul and I decided to postpone the tour for one year.

It turned out to be a wise, even directed decision. Vic was picked to tour India with the England team, so he would have been unavailable. Furthermore, the proposed dates would have clashed with the assassination of Indira Ghandi when the whole of India came to a halt. We should have been unable to do anything.

England in India

Instead it was proposed that I should travel out to India in January 1985, link up with Robin Paul and travel with the England team to Hyderabad, Madras and Bangalore.

This first visit again emphasised the need for, and the opportunity of, ministry within sport. Robin and I arrived in Hyderabad where we were cordially greeted by the Rev. Francis Sunderaj and his family, and immediately made welcome by the England team and management. On the first evening one of the England players, whom I had never met, came up to me at a reception and asked, "What is a born-again Christian?" Another wanted some help with reading the Bible, and all were friendly.

During those three weeks we made contacts which served us well nine months later. In Hyderabad we met P. R. Mansingh, secretary to the Hyderabad Cricket Association, and I agreed to arrange the itinerary for a visit to England by a Hyderabad under-19 XI in return for hospitality to our team. In Madras we linked up with Bharath Reddy, captain of the Tamil Nadu state side. One of that side and a friend of both Bharath and Robin was Paul Moses, a committed Christian. The Tamil Nadu team planned to visit England in June 1985, but they needed someone in England to tie up the loose ends and organise games. It was no trouble for me to do that, and with this reciprocal arrangement we cemented our friendship.

But perhaps the most significant contact of all was the one we made in Bangalore with the Spastics Society of India. For some time the Society had been hoping to stage a large sporting occasion to raise their profile and funds. It was agreed that at least one game would be played for the Society in Bangalore and that we should be the guests of the Society.

Achieving this "deal" involved roaring around the city on the back of Robin Paul's motor-bike. It's a good way to see India. Waiting at a level (but very bumpy) crossing, a crowd of beggars and lepers quickly assembled; queuing at the Bank of India to meet Test player Roger Binny – a long wait rewarded only by the information that "he's at the nets". Half an hour later, dusty and bounced, there was no sign of Roger. Next stop was a wealthy industrialist friend. This was another world, a chaotic office with a

"Mr Big" surrounded by a battery of telephones; all were ringing, but none actually linked you with anyone! We went on to an American missionary's home.

"He's living by faith," Robin said with a rather quizzical look in his eyes.

I anticipated primitive accommodation, probably like Robin's flat – two or three rooms in a stable-block where he lived with his wife, their three children, his mother and his brother's family and sundry livestock. But "living by faith", it seems, involves no such privations. The "missionaries" lived in a large, airy, detached house on the edge of the city.

We drove about 250 miles that day and laid the basis for our visit later. Staying with Robin Paul's parents-in-law, I discovered again that mosquitoes have a built-in preference for European blood. It is probably all that they have in common with West Indian fast bowlers.

England won the one-day international in Bangalore next day. It was a glimpse of what can happen at Indian cricket matches. When it seemed as if India were doomed, fires broke out in the half-completed stands. Gavaskar, the Indian captain, took his team off the field and play was only resumed after a half-hour delay.

To one used to the polite applause of an English cricket ground, the enthusiasm and knowledge of an Indian crowd are very startling. Nine months later we were to have closer experience of it.

Returning to England I had the task of raising the team and the money for the air fares to and from India. Gradually the selection of the team took care of itself. Money was more of a problem. We negotiated good terms with Air India, and raised a substantial amount through Christians in Sport's supporters, by then up to about 1,200 people. But we were still short and I had to ask as many of the players as were able to raise as much as they could themselves. One way or another we made it.

The tour was programmed to begin on Friday, October

18th. We would fly to Bangalore via Madras, arriving on Saturday in time for a full programme of speaking engagements on the Sunday, and the "big match" for the Spastics Society on the Monday.

Unfortunately, there was just one more hitch . . .

The Visas

Everybody who visits India requires a visa. Visitors apply for a visitor's visa and, apart from the long wait at the High Commission of India in Aldwych, it is a straightforward business.

One of our members, Steve Wookey, was resident in Paris and he acquired his visitor's visa without difficulty.

We applied in May, stating a "cricket tour" as the reason for our visit. Unfortunately, the final names of the team were not confirmed until the end of September. Simon Hughes contacted us then and Vic Marks, mercifully, was omitted from the England team to tour the West Indies. By Monday, October 14th, despite repeated requests and reassurances that all would be OK ("no problem"), we had no visas and our passports were in the possession of the High Commission.

The Indian High Commission is a microcosm of Indian life – in other words it is a glorious, endearing, infuriating shambles! I spent most of the next three days there trying to find out what was going on. By this time numerous churches and individuals were praying that somehow we should get our visas. We drafted in the cavalry, Alan Godson, coming down on Wednesday to see what he could do. I arrived back in Oxford that night convinced that there was no way we could go. Our application for visas was in Delhi, and apparently the processing might take three months! Indian officials were very suspicious of England teams following the drunken behaviour of some footballers from the north-east of England who had recently toured India. There was also the South African issue looming. The Commonwealth ministers' meeting was actually in session in Bermuda and Indian officials were screening every sportsman's passport for any sign of the dreaded South African stamp. Furthermore, Christian missionaries were finding it very hard to get visas renewed.

There were "good" reasons for stopping us, it seemed. But probably what happened was simply that the applications were lost in the pile of Indian red tape in Delhi. Pull the right thread, though, and it is surprising how quickly the knottiest problems are solved.

On Thursday, October 17th, they were still shaking their heads in Aldwych. This can be a confusing signal from an Indian because it can mean "yes", but not on this occasion. At lunch-time Alan and I collected the passports and prepared to leave the building. What followed proved to me that God wanted this tour to go ahead.

As we got to the main hallway we were approached by a smiling Indian official.

"Can I help you, gentlemen?" he asked. Now nobody in India House had said that to us before.

As usual Alan reacted more quickly than I. "We want to see the High Commissioner," he said flatly.

"Come this way, please." We were shown into the epicentre of the building. Delhi was rung, action would be taken, we should have to wait, but there was hope.

The flights were postponed and all the players put on "pause". Friday morning was one of the longest of my life. When we should have been flying eastwards, I was pacing our tiny office waiting to hear from the High Commission. At 1 p.m. our time the office was closing in Delhi. If we heard nothing by then I should have to cancel the tour. I busied myself preparing a press release announcing the cancellation. Guy McDonnell rang and I told him to head back to Cambridge from London. At 12.55 Mary, my secretary, persuaded me to ring India House once more.

"Your visas have been cleared," said a voice.

Working frantically, Nigel Freeman, Duncan Martindale and myself managed to get the passports stamped and rearrange flights with the harassed but helpful staff of Air India. All was set for a Sunday morning departure.

Exhausted, I returned to Oxford to telephone the team and ensure that they got to the airport on time. At 10 p.m. on the Saturday my mother rang. Dad had suffered a stroke and had been rushed to hospital. It looked as if I should not be going to India after all.

5

Playing Back

The India Tour

Fortunately, in the morning my father was comfortable, the stroke having been only mild. He was not in danger and the rest of the family insisted that I should go.

So the team assembled at the airport. As we awaited our call to board, Vic looked round at his new team-mates and said, "Oh well, I expect we'll all come back Hindus!"

That week had taught me a great deal about the importance of prayer. Everything that could be done to secure visas had been done. Human effort and time had no effect on Indian bureaucracy; but no human agency can frustrate the power of prayer. I firmly believe that the concerted prayers, offered to God by the members of the team and their home churches, perhaps especially the Christian people at St Aldate's and St Matthew's in Oxford, secured those visas.

Though more exhausted and stressed than I have ever been in my life, I got to that Air India flight to Bombay more sure than ever before that I was doing what God wanted me to do. In *Chariots of Fire* Eric Liddell, the Scottish sprinter, said that he could feel God's pleasure when he ran. God had made him fast. I felt God's pleasure as we soared away from London on our adventure for cricket and for Christ.

Somewhere over the Middle East the captain's voice came over the loudspeaker. "A passenger is seriously ill. We are making an emergency landing." On landing at

Bahrain he came on again. "The passenger has died . . . we must remove the body." A stretcher appeared and a corpse was removed from the plane. Quickly I checked the team. Were they all still there? Who could we afford to lose? I just hoped it wasn't Paul Fisher . . . after all, we only had one wicket-keeper! But they were all alive and well.

On arrival at Bombay there was another announcement, "Would the Reverend Digby report to the airport authority." My heart sank! Was it my father in trouble? Had the visas been withdrawn? What else could happen? To my utter joy and delight there was Robin Paul with the airport authorities. He had flown up to Bombay and arranged everything. Our flight was re-routed and we were going straight to Bangalore. Within two hours we were being garlanded by the welcoming committee at Bangalore airport and reunited with Nigel and Rosemary Freeman, who had travelled out twenty-four hours earlier.

Bangalore

By now it was Monday morning and so we had missed the speaking engagements in churches which Robin had arranged for us on the previous day. Eddie Waxer, just arrived from Florida, and Nigel and Rosemary had done their bit in our absence.

In fact none of us was up to much at all after seventy-two hours of uncertainty and travelling. We all collapsed into bed in the Taj Hotel and contemplated the prospect of playing an Indian Test XI in twenty-four hours' time.

Jack Bond put us through our paces at the stadium that afternoon. Everyone was glad to be playing cricket at last. We had little hope of winning the game and Vic and Jack feared an embarrassing defeat. It would hardly be surprising. No Test team would be asked to play at such a

high level so soon after arrival. It would be a severe
examination for our young and inexperienced players.

We met that evening as a team to study the Scriptures
and pray together. In an article in *The Times* during the
1986 season Graham Cowdrey was to recall how much
these evening devotional times meant to him. On the
first occasion Eddie spoke of his vision for sports ministry
and encouraged us in our role as ambassadors for Christ.

"The day of the big match dawned bright and sunny" –
as they say. I am grateful to journalist Mark Thomas for
his description of that day's events.

There was an atmosphere of expectancy in the city;
35,000 tickets had been reported sold for the team's
game against India. It had been advertised through
newspapers and hoardings arranged by Rotaract on
behalf of the Spastics Society. But the Indian players,
after their defeat at the hands of the Sri Lankans in the
recent Test Series, were determined not to taste any
more cricketing hemlock . . .

They defeated and comprehensively outplayed the
Ambassadors. Batting first, they scored 242 for 9 off 40
overs. Then they drilled out their jet-lagged opponents
who could reply with only 192 for 8 against Sivaramakrishnan and Yadav in front of 12,000 people.

But we did bat and field well. Unfortunately a bus-
driver's strike reduced the size of the crowd.

In fact we were far from disgraced, and the day was
deemed a success by all concerned. Major pluses for us
had been the bowling of Mark Frost and a splendid
innings by Paul Fisher.

There was time for only a quick shower. Despite very
little sleep and a hard game in great heat, the whole team
turned up for a youth rally of young Indian Hindus
and Christians at 6 p.m. Steve Wookey spoke to an
enthusiastic audience. From there we were rushed to a
Modi-Xerox reception for both teams. Each member of

the team took his role as an "ambassador for Christ" very seriously.

I was very thrilled when one of the Indian players came up to me and said, "Andrew, your team is different. They start conversations and seem interested in our country and in us. With most visiting teams we have to make a real effort to make conversation."

There was no brash evangelism going on, but our exhausted team was exhibiting Christian friendship and concern and it was not going unnoticed.

I was approached by an Indian girl and asked for advice. She was a Christian and deeply in love with a Hindu man – a fine young chap to whom she introduced me – what should she do? I pointed out that the Bible teaches us the importance of marrying a fellow believer. She acknowledged the sadness in their relationship because he could not share what was the most important thing in her life. Quietly, in the middle of that busy reception we prayed together that God would guide them, and show them the way forward.

So our first two days in India came to an end. I have gone into detail because it demonstrates so clearly that God can and wants to use sporting talent for His purpose. This group of Christian cricketers was discovering, on active service, what it means to be a Christian in sport. Because of cricket we were being accorded great respect and provided with overwhelming hospitality. Because of cricket our religious convictions were being noticed. Because of cricket we were being consulted about personal issues in people's lives. What possible qualifications did I have to advise an unknown Indian girl about her matrimonial affairs? I was involved in that situation and able, I hope, to help, simply because God had given me an ability to play cricket, and I had made that ability available to Him.

Sport is a wonderful way of getting to know people. Used for God, it can be a mighty vehicle for showing His love and spreading His kingdom.

Our next game was a less-pressurised affair against Bangalore YMCA, playing on a matting wicket and with an outfield of bumpy ground and tufted grass. Vic took one look at it and volunteered to join me in a broadcast for the Far East Broadcasting Association. Our total of 220 owed much to a brilliant innings of 127 by Graham Cowdrey. Only a fiery spell from Mark Frost stopped the YMCA from getting near the target.

That night there was an extraordinary reception at another big hotel in Bangalore. It was a Goanese evening and there were various entertainers from Goa there. We were given the VIP treatment and were warmly welcomed by pop singers and hotel managers, etc. The food was very good, and we were able to sit at a table together and have a slightly more relaxing team meal. After a while the pressure came from the MC for the evening for the English cricketers to dance with any girls they could find at the "do". Fortunately, one or two of our chaps were brave enough to do this, but we soon made a hasty retreat.

Ooty

Friday was an exhausting day; we left early in the morning to travel to a game sanctuary. Unfortunately, our excellent guide, Ravi from the Rotaract group in Bangalore, was anxious that we should see everything possible on the way. It was all very interesting, stopping at a wayside shop for coconut juice, at the summer palace of a noted sultan and for a lengthy stay at Mysore, where we had a guided tour of the palace. However, we then had to drive for a couple more hours to get to the game sanctuary, arriving around 10 p.m. when everyone was feeling pretty tired. We stayed in various log-cabins in comfortable beds but fairly primitive conditions until about 5.30 Saturday morning when we were taken in the back of lorries to search for game in the sanctuary.

After breakfast it was on to Ootacamund. This was the place where C. T. Studd was pastor for six years just after the turn of the century. Ooty is now often referred to as Little England and is right at the top of the Nilgiri hills, 7,000 feet above sea-level. We went up through pine forests and clouds and eventually emerged in a typical Indian town, but one much frequented by Europeans. The climate was much cooler and the welcome at a Christian hostel very warm. We were staying again in very comfortable accommodation, but without particularly European washing facilities! Barry Jenkins, the local pastor at the Union Church where "C. T." had been pastor in bygone years, was there to welcome us and his Australian enthusiasm quickly infected all the party.

C. T. Studd

I suppose C. T. Studd was a prototype of Christians in sport. Norman Grubb has written a classic biography (published by Lutterworth). Charlie Studd had been born into the privileged circles of the British aristocracy in the mid-1860s. He was brought up in a Christian environment, but thought "religion was a Sunday thing like one's Sunday clothes, to be put away on Monday morning . . . we were brought up to have a sort of religion . . . it was just like having a toothache". But in 1877 Charlie's father was converted to Christ after attending an Evangelistic rally at which D. L. Moody spoke. In due course, while a schoolboy at Eton, C.T. "got down on his knees and said thank you to God . . . I knew then what it was to be born again, and the Bible which had been so dry to me before became everything."

A brilliant cricket career followed – Cambridge and England. He played in the historic Test Match at the Oval in August 1882 when the *Sporting Times* announced that "the ashes of English cricket would be taken to

Australia". For two consecutive seasons C. T. Studd was acknowledged as "the premier all-round cricketer in the country".

But gradually a crisis emerged in his life. He became gripped by the truth of Christianity and a desire to introduce others to Christ. He joined the China Inland Mission and in 1885 was one of the famous Cambridge Seven that set sail for missionary work in that most hostile of countries. He had given away his entire fortune, investing instead, as he put it, in "the Bank of Heaven". He worked flat out in China for ten years, nearly killing himself with the magnitude of his labours.

After a period of recovery, and an exhausting preaching tour of North America, he returned to the mission field. This time to Ootacamund. After six years there he prepared for the "great work" of his life – eighteen years in the heart of Africa. It was there in 1931 that he died. Mr Harrison – a colleague – movingly describes his death.

> He had become so weak and exhausted . . . that his voice began to weaken. We got very little of what he was saying . . . he ceased to try to talk about anything and with each little breath he could spare he could only say "Hallelujah! Hallelujah!" It was amazing to see him passing out like this – quite conscious all through and just "Hallelujah" coming with every breath he had . . . at about 7 p.m. he seemed to lapse into unconsciousness and shortly after 10.30 p.m. passed to his reward. It was a fine going.

He was a great man.

The jungles where we had searched unsuccessfully for a tiger were the very same as eighty years before Studd had walked with the Gospel, seeking souls to save. The streets of Ootacamund were probably much the same as they had been in his day. As we drove into Ooty and later, as we walked round, I could not help being thrilled at the thought of treading, with a Christian cricket team, in the footsteps of so great a pioneer.

Of course there were new buildings and some modern conveniences, but in character and essence the place was unchanged. Barry Jenkins told us how children were sacrificed on the completion of these buildings. The average Indian is overwhelmingly courteous and hospitable, but in his country, especially in the rural areas, there are still hideous remnants of paganism. The people are in fear of evil spirts, witchcraft and sorcery. Religious activity is often very superstitious, and just occasionally you come across gross evil like these child sacrifices. Men like C.T. Studd and many before him brought the light of Christ into these dark places. Of course, many mistakes were made, but the light shines out, and is as desperately needed as ever.

Triumph and disaster

An afternoon match had been arranged against a local Nilgiri district team. We were driven to a local school, and shown the ground. It was totally bare of grass, a huge basin carved out of the hillside. On one side on a large bank sat thousands of enthusiastic school-children. Among them I spotted three splendid elderly ladies, sitting beneath their parasols, beaming at all around – an anachronistic symbol of both Raj and early missionary adventure, but a delight to meet.

In the centre of this amphitheatre was a matting wicket on which we compiled 240 in our 30 overs. John Knight delighted the crowd with some spectacular 6-hitting. Opening the bowling, I was again unable to take my first wicket. This was no surprise to me. The matting provided a true surface, and our spin-bowlers, Marks and Dewes (generously flighted leg-spin), did the damage, bowling the local team out for little more than 100. Play was suspended for a while when a cow strayed on to the ground, and again when the Rev. Stephen Wookey sprained his ankle attempting to field a ball which had already gone over the boundary.

Poor chap, he was very sore and unable to play for at least a week. This presented us with an unexpected crisis because, while in Bangalore, we had agreed to send John Knight and Steve to represent England in a double-wicket competition, near Calcutta, in a testimonial for a retiring Indian cricketer. After much discussion and prayer, we decided that Dewes must replace Wookey. They would miss the Coimbatore part of our tour and rejoin us in Madras.

A sprained ankle might prevent Steve from playing cricket, but he made up for it next morning as we put him through an exhausting preaching schedule – four work-outs before lunch! I am glad he managed to climb in and out of each pulpit without further injury.

Most of us went down to the Union Church to attend the two morning services. I spoke at the early service at 10 a.m. and Peter Swaffield at the 11 a.m. morning prayer. It was thrilling that over 100 people – most of them youngsters with years ahead of them – responded to the invitation to commit their lives to Christ.

Ootacamund is the home of Hebron School, a famous boarding-school for children of many nationalities – many are the children of missionaries. The headmaster and staff welcomed us to lunch, and two of them humiliated Frost and Hughes on the tennis court during the afternoon.

At the evening service at the Union Church Vic Marks spoke of his own Christian commitment and was honest about the struggles he faced as a professional cricketer and a Christian. After the sermon twenty or twenty-five stood to commit their lives to Christ. I prayed that for all these people our visit would have provided a stimulus to their faith. India needs its young people to grow up with integrity and drive. There is so much inefficiency, wastage and corruption, and many young people shrug

their shoulders in despair. Robin Paul wanted us to urge
them to be excellent for Christ. Many Christian leaders
like Robin long to see men and women with firm
Christian faith and standards becoming leading lawyers,
doctors, politicians, businessmen, teachers and so on. It
is not easy for the Christian to go against the tide of
corruption, but it can be done. In Bangalore we had met a
Christian police chief who had reached the top and kept
his hands clean, winning the respect of all . . . but it had
been a lonely road he had travelled.

After church that Sunday evening we had been invited
to a party with a difference. Probably only a man with
Barry Jenkins's outrageous enthusiasm could have got
English professional cricketers, the local district team,
Union Church members, and the staff of Hebron School
crawling around on the floor pretending to be animals!
After a while a few of us slipped away leaving Swaffield
and Cowdrey to look after our interests. Apparently
Barry Jenkins suggested another game, the winner of
which would receive a prize of a chocolate bar. This was
too much for Graham who grabbed the microphone and
introduced Peter Swaffield as a musical entertainer.
What followed is still a talking-point in Ootacamund.
Peter successfully imitated as many rock stars as he could
think of, starting a new song every time Barry threatened
another game. Graham, whose devotion to Van Morrison is a byword, found a new hero in the assistant
minister of Upton Vale Baptist Church in Torquay.

Coimbatore

Next morning, Monday, we drove down the tortuous
road from Ootacamund to Coimbatore, where we met
Roger Knight and Rachel Swaffield, who were joining us
for ten days. Once again we were overwhelmed by the
courteous welcome of the people of Coimbatore. I had
never envisaged so rapturous a welcome when I planned

the tour. Two matches had been arranged. A warm-up
game fifty kilometres from the town against a district XI
and a day–night match at Coimbatore for which 37,000
tickets had been sold.

At about 7.30 on Tuesday morning my exhausted team
climbed into a bus taking us to a place called Udamalpet
where we were assured we should have a fairly easy
match, and be joined by Paul Moses. Both seemed like
very good news.

As we approached the town an hour and a half later we
were surprised at the large numbers of people walking
down the streets, and even more surprised when we
drove under a huge banner welcoming the English
Ambassadors Cricketers. We were completely speech-
less when we were shown into the ground . . . 12,000
people were already crammed into stands especially
erected for the match, and on the outfield the Indian Test
team were warming up . . .

Immediately to our left as we looked out on this
colourful scene was the ladies' stand in front of which
Simon Sutcliffe was to field. Vic felt that it would be wise,
in view of the strength of the opposition and the size of
the crowd, if we agreed to bowl first, thus ensuring, we
felt, a full day's entertainment. On a matting wicket with
a treacherous outfield we restricted the Indians to 232 for
9 in 40 overs. I am glad to report that I took a wicket. It
turned out to be the only one of the tour!

In front of the ladies' stand, Sutcliffe – tall, slim,
elegant in his Oxford University cap – dived left and
right, pulling off amazing stop after amazing stop. The
women in their silk saris and with their husbands
situated on the other side of the ground, could barely
contain themselves. At the end of the game he was
awarded the "best fieldsman" prize – a very popular
decision.

We had to get 233 to win after lunch, and were well on
our way thanks to Cowdrey (80) and Moses (100). Only 7
were needed off the last two overs with 6 wickets in

hand. But things began to go wrong. As the last over began Marks had strike and 3 runs were required and 4 wickets remaining. We were confident – our experienced Test cricketer was facing. His last three innings in Test cricket – for England against Pakistan – had all been over 50. We were wondering where he would pick up the 3 runs needed, when he was clean bowled first ball. Fisher went in – our in-form keeper – and missed the second ball, but the wicket-keeper fumbled it. Richardson, backing up, called for a run, but was sent back fatally.

Next in was me – hardly the man for this sort of crisis! Fisher kicks the third ball away, and I manage the same with the fourth. The scores are level, we need 1 to win. We agree to run come what may, but when Fisher misses the fifth ball he sends me back and I am run out. Off the last ball, the ever-popular Sutcliffe is also run out and India have snatched a remarkable victory. Four wickets fell in that last over as we collected a mere 2 runs!

The 12,000 Indians were delighted with the day's proceedings. Moses, the man of the match, donated his prize to the local orphanage, and I was invited to address the crowd. I expressed my hope that they were impressed by the way in which we had so skilfully avoided winning the game, and explained why we were there, thanking them for their hospitality.

It was a great day's cricket and an experience that none of us will ever forget. But as we assembled for dinner on the hotel roof that evening we were all disappointed to have lost, when it seemed impossible that we should do so.

The "Big Match"

Most alarming of all, though, was the news that our captain was ill and had retired to bed. Sure enough, next morning Vic had a high fever, and had been sick all night. This was the day of the "big match". We hoped that he would be fit for start of play at 4 p.m. The rest of us spent a quiet morning at the Coimbatore Club – an outpost of the Raj – playing snooker and swimming.

At 2.30 p.m. a police escort and the Indian team arrived at the club and we were driven to the football stadium where the match was to be played. Some 10,000 were locked outside the ground and 37,000 enthusiastic spectators packed inside. A special turf wicket had been carefully prepared, and played very well. We changed in a tiny room which was also a telephone exchange. Simon Hughes appointed himself chief operator, but seemed to make little contact with the numerous Tamil enquirers who rang through.

We took the field, led by a very morose Marks, amid deafening noise. Now, without doubt, from a cricketing point of view this was the high point of our tour. Never before had Coimbatore staged an international cricket match, and never before, I think, had a game been played under lights in South India. Most of the Indian Test team were lined up against us. Unfortunately, my own memories of the game are tarnished by what followed. I can only give you a biased personal account.

The Indian openers, Srikkanth and Reddy, blazed into Frost and Hughes. I was fielding on the boundary – third man for Hughes and long-on for Frost. Occasionally the ball was blasted over my head, but basically it was very quiet. Marks bowled 3 overs, and I came in from the third-man boundary so could at least hear my colleagues when they shouted at me. Marks withdrew – 0 for 31 off 3 overs and sunstroke! Cowdrey came on to bowl – 8 overs, 0 maidens, 89 runs, 3 wickets . . . hardly tight, I thought. Roger Knight had taken over the captaincy, bowling his overs relatively economically. Sutcliffe turned his arm over. Behind me the crowd shouted, "What number do you bat, sahib?" I held up ten fingers. "Do you bowl?"

"Yes," I shouted back, but they did not believe me, and I didn't really believe it either. Cowdrey bowled the last over. Off the fifth ball I caught a high catch coming out of the floodlights. I was rather pleased with it. Next ball I dropped a slightly harder catch, partly because my feet got stuck in the sand covering the step which separated the football pitch from the athletics track that surrounded it. Cowdrey seemed dismayed.

"It would have been my fourth wicket," he said.

"Four for millions," I replied stroppily as we went back to the telephone exchange.

The Indians had totalled a massive 280. Even with Vic we would have had little chance, and when Knight went cheaply we were batting only for respectability. Fifties from Cowdrey, Martindale and Moses secured that and in the end we were all out for 269 – a very creditable effort. My own contribution to the game consisted in a single to mid-wicket off leg-spinner Sivaramakrishnan, before being bowled blocking Gundappa Viswanath, who, I was told later, had not bowled for ten years!

We were soundly beaten, but the game had been a spectacular success, with 37,000 people paying up to 1,000 rupees for a ticket meant that at least 300,000 rupees went to the Spastics Society.

I returned, silent in the coach to the hotel, and went up to visit Vic. As I laid my tale of woe before him, moaning that I hadn't bowled, he seemed hugely amused and began to recover. I was pleased – more of R.D.V. Knight's captaincy and I should forget how to play!

Strange, isn't it, how even in a team game our individual achievements seem so important?

Paul Moses

The arrival of Paul Moses was proving a great boost to our performances on the field. Paul is a deeply-committed Christian man. He comes from Madras and from a Christian family, but it was not until his early twenties that he finally committed his life to Christ. By then he had made quite a reputation for himself as an all-rounder in

Madras club cricket. But India is a strangely divided country. Religious, geographical and caste differences influence selection for state, zone and Test teams. There is no doubt that Paul's open and firm commitment to Christ has resulted in his often being overlooked for selection. He has accepted this bravely, but before our tour was seriously considering giving up the game. He had recently got married and had his first child and he was beginning to feel that God could not have a plan for him which involved playing the game he loved.

He played quite splendidly for us, and his 100 at Udamalpet gave him and all our team great pleasure. Later he wrote to me that when Vic Marks and Jack Bond congratulated him and praised his cricketing talent it had been the proudest moment of his career.

Christians involved in sport may find that they are viewed with suspicion, and their decision to opt out of some post-match festivities may work against them. In the West it will not be quite so obvious as it has been for Moses in India, but it undoubtedly exists. The Christian may find that he has to be a bit better, or a bit more committed to practice, or a bit more successful than the others to ensure selection.

There is a camaraderie (team spirit is another description) which can quickly become cliquishness in many teams. The man who buys the captain a drink, or leads the expedition to the night-club, or who knows where to find a stripper for the end-of-season dinner binge may find himself more popular with the selectors than the committed Christian.

Of course, it is not always the case. Sometimes the integrity, selflessness and goodwill, which should be characteristics of the Christian sportsman, earn him additional respect from his team-mates. Alan West, Luton Town footballer, was, he remembers, initially viewed with suspicion by his colleagues following his conversion to Christianity, but quickly he found that most respected him for his views and indeed some would come to him for advice and counsel.

One of the great things about being with an all-Christian team in India was that team spirit and mutual concern seemed to come more quickly than in other teams in which I have played. Perhaps it was because we were engaged in a "nobler cause" than simply playing the game.

Madras

This "spirit" survived even the rigours of the seven-hour train journey to Madras. We arrived in the middle of the night to be greeted by a party of Lions Club members who had agreed to look after us during our stay and promote the match against the Indians due to be played on the following Saturday. Like latter-day Daniels, we presented ourselves on the platform. Unfortunately, the "gang" of station porters unloaded our bags on the opposite platform. A furious argument between porters and Lions ensued. In a full-blooded Indian argument any kind of progress seems quite impossible. There is always much shaking of heads and putting of backsides on the floor. Then, equally unpredictably, everything is suddenly no problem. We feared that the odd rupee may have changed hands, but that is only a dark rumour.

Once in the bus we were driven to look at a large poster advertising the game. All our names appeared in glorious technicolour. Well – almost our names. Baptist pastor Peter Swaffield was described as "P. Waffle"; Parisian Anglican clergyman Steve Wookey rejoiced in the name of "T. Wolley" and I was plain "A. Winfield". Our three "Reverend" Ws will never, I am afraid, have quite the same ring as the three West Indian Ws – Weekes, Walcott and Worrell. We also found we had recruited a new, and rather distinguished, possibly

Dutch or German player by the name of Dunken Martyn Dale. We think we have trouble with Indian names!

If ever you go to Madras, be sure to visit Fisherman's Cove. There on the Friday we relaxed, played cricket and enjoyed the glorious sea, sand and hospitality. But not all of us. Some were busy at school assemblies, coaching clinics and church meetings. The professional cricketers especially enjoyed, and were good at, the coaching clinics. They felt more comfortable on this their own territory than in front of a school assembly or church meeting. They were much appreciated by all the schools we visited.

The last of the four one-day matches against the Indian side was scheduled for Saturday, November 2nd. It was a disappointment. We started well, but a magnificent innings of 120 by Sandeep Patel destroyed our bowling. We never got near their total of 280. This was a really strong Indian side, including Kapil Dev, Patel, Gundappa Viswanath, Binny, Strikkanth, Sivaramakrishnan, Venkataraghavan, Vengsarkar, Arun and Akbar Ibraham. They would have given any team in the world a hard game, so they were too good for us!

But what a tremendous thing that such a side had been assembled to play in aid of the Spastics Society! It was another indication of the impact Christian sportspeople can have. Such an event had not happened in India before. It took a visit like ours to provoke it. They even postponed the pre-Australia tour cricket camp for three days to fit us in!

A game against a Madras cricket club had been arranged for the Sunday. I had not wanted any games on Sunday so that we would be free to attend and speak at as many churches as possible, but Robin Paul and the club felt it was right to play and I had agreed. We awoke on Sunday morning to torrential rain. The whole city seemed to be under water. There was no way we could play cricket. This was the only hint of rain during the three weeks. Did God also think it best if we did not play on a Sunday?

We moved out in pairs to the churches who had invited us to speak. We went to Roman Catholic, Church of South India, and Methodist services. At some places we were translated into the Tamil language and at others we spoke in English. Everywhere we were accorded a friendly welcome and listened to attentively.

Hyderabad

Next morning we flew on to Hyderabad for the last leg of the tour. By then Simon Hughes had left us for Perth where he was playing club cricket for the winter, and Roger Knight and Rachel Swaffield returned to their school-teaching duties in England.

Whereas everywhere we had been thus far had been predominantly Hindu, Hyderabad and Secunderabad, which are twin cities, have a large Moslem population. We wondered if this would make our reception more formal, but not a bit of it. The Hyderabad Cricket Association and its secretary, P.R. Mansingh, whom I had met back in January, met us at the airport and provided a coach, a guide and hotel accommodation. They had arranged three matches against local sides. They included several state players and provided excellent opposition. We won two of the games and lost one.

We were also welcomed by the Rev. Francis Sunderaj, a well-known Christian leader in the city. He had arranged for us to speak at school assemblies each morning and at a youth rally one evening. We participated in a meal with the Christian leaders of the city and I spoke at a pastor's seminar about sports ministry.

I am bound to report that at this stage of the tour I succumbed to sunstroke in a last, desperate attempt to return home with a tan. I sat for most of our innings on the Tuesday in the blazing sun. By tea-time I was suffering from a severe headache and nausea and had to retire to bed. I managed to speak at a youth rally that evening, but felt very rough. After my address I invited any who wished to respond to the Gospel to come forward. Robin Paul was encouraging me in this method. No one came and we looked rather foolish. The meeting closed and a teenage boy approached me. There were tears in his eyes as we shook hands.

"God has really spoken to me," he said. Quietly I led him to Christ. We correspond regularly. He was a Hindu, perhaps in a way – culturally at least – he still is, but he has met Jesus and he knows the love of God. After we had prayed that evening I introduced him to Francis Sunderaj and asked that he should look after him when we left.

"You will need the word of God," Francis told him, and presented him with his own, no doubt very expensive, leather-bound Bible. It was a gesture that typified the Indian Christians that we met during the tour.

All the team were thrilled to speak at the school assemblies. We were given a rapturous welcome each time and had the privilege of talking about God's love and the uniqueness of Christ to thousands and thousands of young Hindus and Moslems. Vic and I went to a girls' secondary school, and after we had made our contributions the headmistress invited any of the girls who wished to meet the cricketers to come forward and do so. Immediately we were immersed in a throng of enthusiastic, saried Indian teenagers. I must admit they seemed more enthusiastic about Vic than me, and I shall not easily forget his yell for help, "Andrew, get me out of here!" Later he described it in the *Daily Telegraph* as the fulfilment of his teenage dreams.

And so finally to Bombay for twenty-four hours before our flight home. Cowdrey and Martindale had left for Australia and Wookey for Paris. I took the remnant to see the work of a friend of mine, the Rev. Saba Renjithan, in the shanty towns of Bombay.

Saba

Throughout our time in India we had been given the very best that our hosts could manage. Indians are extremely courteous people; they like their guests to think well of them and make a great effort to ensure that they are comfortable. We had stayed in comfortable hotels, been given countless exotic meals, been taken sightseeing and had even had the secret rooms of Mysore palace opened for us.

But in Bombay we had a glimpse of another India. Of course, we had seen beggars and cripples in the streets, and driven past very primitive dwellings. Saba took us into his "slums". I had been there before and knew what to expect, but to the rest of the team it came as a profound shock. There were 50,000 people living in Anna Nagar, crowded into one square mile. Primitive corrugated-iron and wooden shacks housed whole families. There was no electricity and two toilets for the entire population. Poverty, such as we had never experienced, deprivation and exploitation stared us literally in the face. The men distilled liquor drawn from the filthy water in the sewers running through the place. This they sold on the black

market on the streets of Bombay. The police, it was
alleged, took ninety per cent of their profits as protection
money. In Mathras Wadi people collected paper and
baled it for recycling, earning enough rupees only to
delay starvation and disease.

Most of the slum dwellers are Tamils from the rural
areas down south in search of employment and prosper-
ity in the big city. But life has played a cruel trick on them
and they are now trapped in poverty. There is really no
material hope for these people. The population of India
continues to grow rapidly and the numbers in poverty
rise.

Hinduism teaches that poverty is a just punishment for
an evil life, and if things turn out right, it will be better in
the next life. Of course, the Resurrection of Jesus Christ
utterly contradicts reincarnation. As Christians we believe in resurrection to a new spiritual existence, rather
than reincarnation for another life in this world. The
Christian view is of life after death in heaven; the Hindu
anticipates further forms of earthly existence. This belief
in reincarnation had led to an amusing moment in
Bangalore. One of our team, on his first visit to India, was
perplexed by the cows wandering around the streets. He
asked Eddie Waxer – a more experienced traveller – why
this was, and why Hindus were often vegetarian.

"Would you eat your mother-in-law?" was Eddie's
unhesitating reply.

Joking apart, though, the Hindu commitment to reincarnation can result in a fatalism which accepts poverty,
injustice and corruption. The Christians we met in India
were concerned about these things as well as preaching
the Gospel.

In the midst of this hopelessness of the slums works
Saba. His father was a Hindu teacher and Saba grew up
fiercely opposed to Christianity and all it stood for. Then
as a young man he went to hear a Christian preacher. He
imagined that the preacher would attack Hinduism and
Saba was ready to refute him publicly. But to his surprise

the man never mentioned Hindus nor their religion, but rather spoke of the love of God for all people and the sacrifice of His only Son so that all men might be forgiven and find new life. Saba knew it was true and in due course became a Christian. This cost him his family and friends, but he found much more. In due course, he felt God calling him to work among the poor people of Bombay.

The Methodist church, the denomination of which he is a minister, was sceptical about his work in Anna Nagar slums, but Saba was undeterred. He knelt down in a muddy clearing in the middle of the slum with his wife and began to pray that God would build His church even there and that these poor people would come to know Him. Not surprisingly (this is India) a crowd gathered. As Saba said, "When there was a big crowd, I told them about Jesus."

Former Cambridge University and Sussex cricketer, John Spencer, was introduced to Saba during a cricket tour of India with the boys of Brighton College. John was deeply troubled by what he saw and determined to help. Through the generosity of Brighton College charities a hut was purchased and a primary health clinic established. Saba preached and demonstrated the love of God, a doctor and nurse attended to urgent medical needs.

The first time I went to India I took with me badly-needed medical supplies. By my second visit, Saba had found a hut that could be used for a similar purpose in Mathras Wadi. In the midst of this hell on earth Saba – God's man for that situation – has fanned into life a spark of hope. With financial help, much prayer and Saba's commitment the spark may become a blaze.

We were all touched by the smiling faces of the children, the love of the people for their pastor and the brave faith of the few who have been converted and baptised. Here was Christianity in action.

So we returned from as fascinating and frustating a country as you could ever visit, with contradictory experiences. At one moment we were rubbing shoulders with Test cricketers who are accorded superstar status by an adoring Indian public, and the next seeing a little of the sorrows and joys of Saba's work among the slum dwellers.

Everybody says it and it is true – India is a country of sharp contrasts.

6

Settling In

The Indian experience has been the most ambitious enterprise undertaken by Christians in Sport. It confirmed that Christian sportsmen and sportswomen have a great opportunity of influencing the world for Christ. I returned from India as I had done from America and Hong Kong, convinced of the importance of establishing a strong Christian presence in all our national sports.

The chief problem was the one that Middlesex cricketer Graham Barlow identified clearly for me: how could we make the Christian faith seem relevant to people caught up in the glamour and excitement of top-level sport? Until sportsmen get to know committed Christian people personally, they cannot make any connection between their life style and the Church. So how do we create a situation where they can make Christian friends?

The first major step forward came in the summer of 1984 when I accepted the national executive of Christians in Sport's invitation to move out of parish ministry and into full-time work with Christians in Sport. The rector of St Aldate's Church, Oxford, Michael Green – then a trustee of Christians in Sport – backed up that invitation with another to join the staff of St Aldate's. For family and geographical reasons Oxford seemed a good base.

Once in Oxford, St Aldate's provided a small office in their run-down youth centre – the Catacombs – where on my very first day I bumped into Mary Baynes, who in due course became our full-time secretary.

It's fun to discover how God can provide for us, if we

are doing what He wants. In 1980 I worked for three
months for Christians in Sport between my job as curate
and moving to Hadley Wood. At that time Sue and I
drove a splendid but rather old Morris 1000 (provided by
my brother-in-law, even though he won his bet about my
batting). Working for Christians in Sport would involve a
lot of travel – a Morris 1000 might not be the answer. One
day I took the old car to be serviced at Stephen James
Autos in Finchley – a garage owned by a church member
at Cockfosters, Duncan Collins. I explained my hopes for
the future.

"Can I help?" he asked.

"Well, you could help me find a reliable second-hand
car, I suppose."

"You've got a car. I'll provide you with one."

Since then he has done just that. Without my asking or
expecting, God moved in one of His people's hearts to
prompt him to respond to a need.

So there I was in Oxford, with an office, a secretary, a
car, a church base and, thanks to the generosity of a large
Christian trust, enough money to start operations full-
time.

What then should we do to further God's purposes in
sport? How could we begin to make Christ seem relevant
to sportspeople?

Chaplains

Way back in the early 1970s one of the first people Eddie
Waxer had contacted was the Rev. Michael Pusey, pastor
of Farnborough Baptist church, and later of the Kings
Centre in Aldershot. Mike was the honorary chaplain of
4th Division Aldershot Football Club. People are somewhat surprised to discover that God has a sense of
humour. Aldershot FC might not be the club that the
world would choose to be the starting-point for a
significant development in British sport. On the other
hand, some might argue that Aldershot's need for divine

guidance was more obvious than for other more successful clubs! Anyway, Mike, a football nut, was their
chaplain. He came on the trip to Orlando in 1977 and
determined then to co-ordinate the development of the
chaplaincy programme in football.

In fact we found that one or two clubs also had
chaplains – the Rev. John Jackson had been involved
with Leeds United for a number of years. When he first
arrived he was unsure what to do, and was viewed with
some suspicion by the players. Then one of the players
suffered a bereavement. No one knew what to say to
him, but John went to his house and was able to comfort
and pray with the family. Next morning everybody at the
club knew what had happened, and many of them came
up and thanked John for what he had done. From then
on, they could see that a chaplain had a role, a use, a
purpose. It's interesting to see that many of the Leeds
players who have gone on to management jobs after their
playing days were over have appointed chaplains in their
clubs – a testimony to John Jackson's influence.

Of course, every chaplain is also a local minister. He
earns his bread by his pastoring of his church. His
involvement with sport is a natural extension of his
church duties. Just as he visits local shops, industry, old
people's homes, so he sees his sports club as a legitimate
area of ministry.

A typical example of a good chaplaincy situation
developed at Watford. The Rev. Richard Harbour was
the minister of St James Road Baptist church, just down
the road from the Vicarage Road headquarters of Elton
John's Watford FC. Elton John had appointed a dynamic
new manager to the club – Graham Taylor – and he saw
that if his ambitions for the club were to be realised then
the people of Watford must be encouraged to identify
more closely with their team.

He encouraged the players to live in Watford and
when approached by Richard Harbour, who was also
seeking ways for his church to be more involved in the local

community, approved the idea of an honorary chaplaincy. In fact Richard then largely delegated the work to his enthusiastic and football-mad assistant, John Boyers.

Initially John went into the club once a week to do some training with the "lads". In fact all they let him do at that stage was pop-mobility and the cross-country run. In due course, John convinced them of his undoubted ball skills and he has occasionally played in a 5-a-side practice game. He may have convinced Graham Taylor, but his football ability is still viewed with considerable scepticism by the national executive of Christians in Sport!

More important than training, though, was that John began to get to know the players as friends, and they could see that not every vicar was the tea-sipping twit caricatured on so many television programmes. For many sportsmen and sportswomen in the UK that image is all they know of Christianity or the Church, so it is hardly surprising that they accept the arrival of a chaplain with some hesitation.

Exeter City invited a young Evangelist, Richard Chewter, to be their honorary chaplain. One of his first engagements was to attend the end-of-season stag dinner for the players. It was all a set-up of course. After dinner a lady appeared and proceeded to strip ostentatiously near the new chaplain. Eyes moved from stripper to vicar; how would he react?

"All right then, vic?" shouted one of the players down the tables.

"Fine, thanks," replied Richard, "but you didn't tell me your mother was coming!"

I'm sure that incident broke down a few barriers!

We have found that where a suitable man is available, chaplaincy in sports clubs enables many of the misunderstandings that exist between Christianity and sport to be overcome. Many players have personal problems, or indeed professional crises that they do not wish to share with anyone intimately involved with their working

lives. For instance, marriages are often put under great
stress by the demands of professional sport – a chaplain
can be a real help in listening and, if appropriate,
advising young players.

John Boyers from Watford has written an article about
football chaplaincy in the 1986 *Rothman's Football Year
Book*.

In it he writes:

> In the football world, chaplaincy is not a means of
> achieving a high profile for the chaplain or his church,
> nor is it a way of getting on the board of directors, nor a
> way of getting match tickets. Football chaplaincy is
> simply a way of serving others, supporting those in
> need and helping those under pressure.
>
> Take, for example, the uncertainties facing new
> apprentices at a club. It may be the first time the
> youngsters have left home. The padre can be a friend
> to these lads, to help them through the difficult early
> stages of their career. Or consider a player who finds
> that his career is threatened by injury. When facing a
> major operation, for example, the support of a padre in
> the form of sympathy, care, concern, and even prayer
> is often welcomed. Sometimes, a player may be
> worried about illness in his family, or the fact that a
> baby is about to be born, or he may need to share
> confidentially about something weighing on his mind.
> In all these situations and more, a chaplain can be a
> friend of the club, a sort of pastoral safety net . . . A
> chaplain can add something to the life of a club which
> many regard as beneficial . . . It is not a case of the
> church jumping on soccer's bandwagon, but a genuine
> attempt to serve and support the game and its people
> with compassion and integrity.

Chaplaincy is a long-term way for Christians in Sport to
offer a service to sport and hopefully to introduce
sportspeople to the good news of Jesus Christ.

Fellowship

Jesus said, "where two or three are gathered together in my name, there am I in the midst" (Matt. 18:20 AV). Most Christian sportspeople are lonely, spiritually isolated, and sometimes socially ostracised – often by their own choice. They find it hard to enter into the abandoned social pastimes of the rest of the team because they don't want to get drunk, gamble or be unfaithful to their wives or girlfriends. But equally they find it hard to get involved fully in the fellowship of their local church. Their commitment to their sport, involving training in the evenings, perhaps, or playing on Sundays, may be viewed with some suspicion by other church members. Even if not, then regular attendance at church is virtually impossible because of the demands of travel and competition.

Take a county cricketer like Vic Marks, for example. He will be involved in Sunday League matches virtually every week between the end of April and the middle of September. Sometimes he might get along to a church service in Tiverton before dashing to a home game at Taunton. But his mind might well be on the game ahead. Half the time he arrives at some distant hotel late on a Saturday night after a long day's cricket and a long evening's drive. He could get out of bed and struggle to a strange church, with nobody he knows, but would you?

Come the middle of September, exhausted county cricketers arrive home to their wives and children desperate for a rest and some family time. They will snatch two weeks' holiday and try to get away to the sunshine.

For in October it is time to pack the cricket-bag again and head overseas in search of coaching or playing opportunities. Returning in March to the local church, it is hardly surprising if the minister greets them at the door with the time honoured, "Now I don't think we have met before, have we?"

It is not quite so bad for footballers. Alan West has become a pastor of his church in Luton; Peter Hart, of Walsall, came to faith when he and Liz took their children along to their local church to be baptised. They are fully involved now in its Christian life and witness. Bernard McNally, at Shrewsbury, has publicly expressed his preference for not playing football on Sunday because he and Karen and their three children feel it is a day to be with the Lord's people, and a day of rest. In 1986 Justin Fashanu became an elder at his church in Brighton. But it is significant that that occurred when Justin had sustained a serious knee injury which threatened his career. Professional sport is an all-consuming career that demands total commitment.

Alan Comfort had a major confrontation with his club, Cambridge United, when he defied his manager's request to train on a Sunday morning following a bad run of defeats. Alan affirmed that Sunday morning was his "church time" and he was sticking to it. But a footballer is contracted to do what the club wants twenty-four hours a day, seven days a week. Refusing to train puts him in breach of contract. Shortly afterwards he was transferred to Leyton Orient.

And what of professional tennis players and golfers? All must travel the world endlessly and compete on Sunday if they are to compete at the top level. Athletes, too, have training and "meets" on Sunday . . . often that is the only time coaches are free to spend time with them.

Fellowship is hard to obtain for many top-level sportsmen and sportswomen. And yet fellowship, meeting together with fellow believers is a Scriptural requirement for all Christians. The very first Christians, the disciples of Jesus, met together for fellowship, teaching and prayer. They broke bread together and remembered the death of Jesus on the cross – His body broken and His blood shed for them. The writers of the New Testament saw the spread of Christianity as the growth of a new community – a "new Israel". Christians were for the apostle, Paul, the "body of Christ" – interdependent. "Can the eye say to the foot, 'I have no need of you' . . . ?" We all need one another as Christians. The writer to the Hebrews insisted, "do not neglect to meet together especially as the Day [of Christ's return] draws near" (see Hebrews 10:25).

In Christians in Sport we are aware that there is a crucial need to provide fellowship for sportsmen. This encourages the believers and draws in those on their way to faith.

Area groups

Across the UK there now exists a network of area groups whose object is to provide the fellowship and support which Christian sportspeople need if their faith is to remain vibrant. Each group devises its own format, but most meet about once a month to pray together, share each other's joys and sorrows, and perhaps plan ways of inviting their fellow sportspeople to hear about Jesus.

In many parts of the country these local groups organise dinners or suppers to which they invite their team-mates and friends. After a dinner, speakers – perhaps including a well-known sports personality – explain what Christ means to them, and invite guests to consider their lives before God. Sometimes there is a musical element to the evening. On several occasions Cliff Richard has come along. He has a way of communicating with sportspeople and he experiences the same type of pressures that they do. Gerald Williams has often spoken. They are happy, stylish evenings, sometimes in a hotel restaurant, a church complex or a football or county cricket club. The atmosphere is that of a sports occasion, but the chief guest and the dominant influence is Jesus Christ.

These area groups also provide a support and encouragement to local churches. As Christians in Sport's work and profile increase we have found that more and more churches are trying to reach out into the local sports scene. One way of doing that is by holding a sportsmen's service. Initially, the idea was to invite a well-known sports personality to come and share their faith. This did nothing for the shy and inarticulate Christian sportsmen and sportswomen and we have discouraged such exploitation of them. Instead, a number of local Christians in Sports people, perhaps with somebody well known, come and lead the whole of the service. In this way the player is not left unsupported and exposed.

God is not calling sportsmen to convert England. That is the Church's task. The Christian sportsman as part of the Church has his role, but usually it is not through speaking. He is called by God to compete at the highest level in a way which brings honour and glory to God. He does not want the credit for himself, but for the God who gave him the talent and ability. Any well-known sports personality who lives a life of Christian integrity will attract media attention – so let the media do his preaching for him!

The telephone also provides a crucial link between Christian sportspeople. In an area group, members ring one another to share encouragement and pass on requests for prayer. Players may be absent for long periods of time but the telephone can reach them anywhere, and they can be made to feel wanted and part of the Christian community.

University Groups

Sport plays a large part in university and college life. In the USA the Fellowship of Christian Athletes has had a large impact on the life of college campuses and high schools. Here in England groups along the lines of those which sprang up in Oxford and Cambridge have been formed in several other universities. The sporting students who are Christians find great strength in meeting together, usually each week, to pray and to encourage each other's witness to their team-mates.

For a while the Cambridge University group was led by a hulk of a man called Willie Stileman. Willie is a rugby player and played in the second row for Cambridge University before joining the Harlequins, who play at the famous rugby ground at Twickenham. Not only is Willie a physically big man, but a man of big faith. The impact of his life on the sportsmen of his generation at Cambridge was considerable. For three years he played virtually every club match for the university but was overlooked for selection for the all-important game against Oxford. It is only those who play in the Varsity match who are awarded the coveted blue. By the time his fourth year began – a year in which he trained to be a teacher – Willie had become a great favourite with the Grange Road crowd in Cambridge, and their delight knew no bounds when he was selected for the big match and won his blue.

In the face of three years of disappointment, Willie's witness as a Christian was impressive. Though he longed for a blue and trained and played hard to earn it, he knew that it was not all-important. His sense of self-worth did not depend on his success as a rugby player, but on the knowledge that he was loved by God and secure in his relationship with Christ. Under his leadership the group in Cambridge grew not only in numbers and maturity, but developed in its relationship with local Christians and other Christian societies, most notably the CICCU – the Cambridge Inter-Collegiate Christian Union. Sportsmen are no different from other men and women in that they need fellowship and teaching which ideally a local church provides. The Christian Union in a university or college set-up also provides excellent teaching and fellowship. The Christians in Sport group cannot and must not compete with either.

But sportsmen enjoy one another's company and can be socially hostile with other non-sporting groups. So élitist can they become both at university and at professional level that they are almost unreachable by the local church and Christian Union. So the Christians in Sport group exists to do what other Christian groupings cannot do – contact sportspeople where they are, on their own territory, and encourage them to consider their lives before God.

In Cambridge many students have come to faith in Christ as the Christians in Sport group have prayed for them week by week and expressed God's concern for them by friendship and by passing on the message of the Gospel.

At the end of the day the university, local churches, the Christian Union, to say nothing of the individuals themselves, benefit enormously from the existence of such groups.

Women's golf

During the summer of 1985 three of the ladies competing on the Women's Professional Golf Association European tour began to get together as Christians. The three, Jane Connachan, Alison Nicholas and Kitrina Douglas, came from different parts of the country, different church traditions and denominations, and have very different personalities. They would, I think, not naturally be close friends even though they have golf in common. But they do possess a supernatural bond which the world will never understand nor emulate.

Through their weekly meetings and with the assistance of golf enthusiast Stuart Weir, on behalf of Christians in Sport, their profile as Christians on the tour has greatly increased. Several of the girls on the tour made commitments to Christ and their weekly gathering grew from three to around a dozen within a year.

Their stand as Christians attracted media attention. An American girl competing on the European tour,

Meredith Marshall, told the meeting in Sweden in 1986 that she was stuck in her Christian life and disappointed that she wasn't more effective in her witness as a Christian. She asked the other girls to pray that she would have opportunities to speak out for Christ and be revived in her faith. This they willingly did.

The following week they all turned up at Dalmahoy for the Scottish Open. At the fellowship meeting that week Jane Connachan's saintly Aunt Agnes told of what Christ meant to her. Meredith was deeply moved by Aunt Agnes's example and message and experienced a new peace in her heart such as she had not known for a while. Though she had never won a tournament before, she won the Scottish Open next day by a massive 7-stroke margin. Several national newspapers reported her victory and her clear profession of the Christian faith at the press conference after the tournament. They reported it without cynicism and without bias – Meredith Marshall attributed her success to the peace she experienced in Christ.

In a short week her cry for help in Sweden had been abundantly answered.

At the end of the 1986 season, Christians in Sport organised a small outreach event in Gerrards Cross to coincide with the Laing Classic at Stoke Poges. I went along and was able to lead two golfers to Christ in just a few hours. The effect of the Christian lives of these golfers, and the power of prayer, were plain to see.

Cricket

Inevitably my own love for the game and involvement in it mean that there are plenty of opportunities in professional cricket.

I have discovered that time spent with Christian cricketers at county matches is never wasted. The relatively slow pace of cricket means that there is plenty of opportunity to chat with players – be they Christians or not. I have already recounted how Alan Knott could use my visits to the Kent dressing-room as a way of initiating discussion on Christian things. Perhaps because quite a few players know me, perhaps because cricket is that sort of game, but often there will be opportunity to speak of the Lord. Many sportsmen have some faith, they know that their talent is a "given" thing, and they do not so much need leading to faith as educating about the God they already believe in. This is strikingly so with many of the West Indian players in county cricket.

I recall going up to the Oxford University Parks one lovely Saturday in May 1986 when Kent were playing the university. We decided to make a family outing of it. As we strolled across the front of the pavilion our daughter Anna (then aged six) spotted Mary – the Christians in Sport secretary – sitting with Graham Cowdrey and Eldine Baptiste. Graham had told Eldine who Anna was and he later asked her if she would be going to church the next day.

"Yes, to St Matthew's," was Anna's reply.

"Could you say a prayer for me?" asked Eldine.

"I'll pray for you now", popped in Anna to her eternal credit . . .

"Dear Lord, please help Eldine to score lots of runs, Amen."

A wicket soon fell and Eldine went in and made 100!

Many of these West Indians have grown up in Christian families, where church-going was the rule. Viv Richards has often spoken and written of his childhood in the local church choir in Antigua. Middlesex and England opening batsman Wilf Slack has recently returned in open commitment to the faith with which he grew up.

But even with players from this and other countries which make up the so-called "post-Christian world" there is a lurking awareness that there is someone out there. I have met only one or two well-known sportsmen and sportswomen who would call themselves atheists or agnostics. What the great majority have not yet had shown to them is that the "great power" out there became a helpless, puking baby in a stinking stable in the Middle East, born of an unmarried mother and slain after thirty-three years by an unconcerned Roman governor, and mourned by only eleven men and a handful of women.

Sportsmen live on an ego trip, so they find it rather offensive to believe in so great an act of self-denial. We should not be surprised that they find it hard.

And yet, increasingly, around the world well-known sports stars are being convinced.

Rod Headley, the old Worcestershire and West Indies cricketer and son of one of the greatest of all batsmen, George Headley, once told me with tears in his eyes, "Andrew, my friend, there are many Christians playing sport, you know, but they just don't know it yet. What Christians in Sport can do is help them to know the Lord for themselves. He means so much to me."

Ron is a lovely man – a great talker about the game, and a loyal member of the Christians in Sport group in the West Midlands. There, because of his predictably bad time-keeping he is known affectionately as "our late brother Headley".

The Commonwealth Games

The Games of 1986 were held in Edinburgh and the churches of Edinburgh invited Christians in Sport to be involved in ministry to the athletes in the competitors' village. Working with the official chaplains, we were able to befriend and encourage many of the athletes from different Commonwealth countries.

Ron Moncur had come from Canada to Edinburgh to compete in the 48kg category in the wrestling. Ron had been to Bible college, but felt that God wanted him to use his athletic talent as a vehicle for sharing the Gospel. In Edinburgh he won a gold medal and spoke at an open-air service in Princes Street to a congregation of 1,000. Linda Spenst – another Canadian – later wrote saying how thrilled she had been that through the contact with Christians in Sport in Edinburgh she had been able to use her talent as a heptathlete to tell people about Jesus.

Bigboy Matlepeng had come all the way from Botswana to run in the marathon. The *Daily Mail* featured a long article about his Christian faith and I went along to the Botswana accommodation to meet him. Bigboy – yes, that really is his name – gripped my hand eagerly. "You are a minister, come to see *me*? Oh, thank you."

We only had a few minutes together but it was joy to be with such a brother. He came in about tenth in the marathon (a very creditable performance considering the cold winds and wet weather that prevailed in Edinburgh that week). To my amazement Bigboy ran the last leg of the 4×400 metre relay for the Botswana team on the day after the marathon – he won a great cheer from the crowd as he came in.

Overseas visits

The international nature of sport means that the UK is often visited by athletes from all over the world.

Right back in the early days the Christian tennis players visiting Wimbledon every June provided an annual stimulus to our ministry. Many times players like Margaret Court, Stan Smith, Gene and Sandy Meyer, Nduka Odiza, Wendy White and Mike Leach have spoken about their commitment to Christ at sportsmen's services and Christians in Sport events.

Dennis Ralston has spoken of how he came to faith through the witness on and off the court of Stan Smith. Gerald Williams describes his conversion in *A Whole New Ball Game*.

Another of Stan Smith's virtues is his unflappability, and it was this, tested beyond most men's endurance, that once led to a life-changing experience for another champion, Dennis Ralston. It happened in 1972. Dennis Ralston was captain of the United States team due to play Rumania in (of all places) Bucharest in what used to be called the challenge round of the Davis Cup. To have to play Ilie Nastase and Ion Tiriac, at their peak, on a slow clay court in their own country was just about the most daunting prospect any team could face, but the American team of Smith, Tom Gorman and Eric van Dillen flew into the Romanian capital ready to do just that.

Impartial witnesses to what happened in that match even today find themselves enraged by the memory of the behaviour on and round the court. They recall that the neutral referee, Enrique Morea, admitted that he was afraid for his life, the crowd were so violently partisan. Some people who were there believe that had Morea taken the kind of disciplinary action he should have done, there could have been serious disorder.

In that incendiary atmosphere, the final began with Nastase playing Smith. It was Nastase's city, Nastase's kind of court, certainly not Smith's. But Smith won that match 11–9, 6–2, 6–3. One–nil to the United States.

In the second singles, Tiriac then beat Gorman in five sets. That made it 1–all. Next, in the doubles Smith and van Dillen beat Nastase and Tiriac in three sets. 2–1 to the United States. But Dennis Ralston knew that Smith would have to beat Tiriac in the next match if America were to win, because the fifth rubber was between Nastase and Gorman, and Gorman had never beaten Nastase in seventeen previous meetings.

It was all up to Stan Smith, and, from his captain's chair at the side of the court, while the crowd howled and abused, and some of the line-calling almost drove the American players to distraction, Dennis Ralston could only sit there, powerless, gripped with tension, and watch.

Well, the records show that Smith beat Tiriac 6–0 in the fifth set. Ralston remembers that it was "absolutely unbelievable".

Now this happened at a period in Dennis's life when he was vaguely conscious that all was not well within him. He had been a professional tennis player a long time – Wimbledon singles finalist against Manuel Santana back in 1966 – and all the travelling had taken its toll on him. What had helped, no doubt, to bring him to this point of awakening was the fact that his wife, Linda, had already become a Christian, and he had been sensitive to the change in her life.

Sitting there near the umpire's chair through the torrid battles of Bucharest, Dennis Ralston recognised "that Stan Smith had something I certainly didn't". So he made a point of talking to him after the tie was finished, talking of deep things, and he began to have some inkling of the source of Stan's security.

"After we got back to the States," Dennis recalls, "I went four nights running to hear an evangelist at Linda's church, Porter Barrington. He talked about steps to salvation, but I felt that somehow I couldn't be forgiven. That would be too much to handle – that the slate could be wiped clean."

So in the secret caverns where a man wrestles with his troubled thoughts, Dennis Ralston searched to grasp the full implication of the stupendous claim that Christians make for Jesus Christ; that, somehow, on the bleak cross, at Calvary, cruelly beaten till his flesh was ripped open, rejected and ridiculed, with nails hammered through his hands and feet, He settled for all time the massive debts of generations past, present and future.

So simply that it was a truth too massive properly to comprehend, man had merely to accept, by an act of faith, that he was made "not guilty" and live in obedience to that light. Dennis had only to say "yes", and he did. Today he is one of the most mature Christians in the tennis world.

From time to time Christian teams from the US come on tours of the UK. In 1985 the Athletes in Action wrestling team had a considerable impact in Strangeways prison in Manchester. The inmates were not accustomed to seeing Christian wrestlers throwing each other around the chapel and talking about the love of Jesus . . . but then, who is?

The following year a team of Christian soccer players toured Europe and spent time in the Manchester and Luton areas. Again their presence and ministry were much appreciated by all they met.

So by promoting fellowship – in all these different ways – seeing the appointment of chaplains, and befriending individual sportsmen and sportswomen wherever we can, Christians in Sport is seeking to bring the love and the relevance of Christ into our sport. It is not easy, often there are disappointments and frustrations . . . but we are on our way.

7

The Loud Appeal

So you like sport . . . I don't suppose you would have got this far in the book if you didn't!

Maybe you are a top performer, striving to achieve the highest accolades – a gold medal, international honours, world records, winners' medals and a cabinet full of trophies. But in your heart, where, as Americans would say, "the rubber meets the road", you are still a plain, ordinary man or woman.

Maybe you are an "honest trier". You love your sport, but, to be honest, you know you'll never be much better than you are today, and that is not very good. But you love it, you really enjoy playing; perhaps your social life revolves around your friends at the golf or tennis club. You follow the achievement of the great ones with wonder. As Severiano Ballesteros drives from the green 300 yards into the distance, you wonder, "maybe one day it'll all come right for me". As Ian Botham hammers sixes in all directions, you think, "he's not doing it that differently from me, why can't I . . . ?" As Diego Maradonna scythes through another line of defensive players, rounds the goalkeeper and thunders the ball into the back of the net, you are dreaming of a hat trick next Saturday afternoon in the park.

Maybe you are an armchair enthusiast . . . we shall all join you in the end! For you, there was never the thrill of scoring goals, dunking baskets, making try-saving tackles, or million-dollar putts. But you have lived through every one in recent years. The America's Cup, The Ashes, Wimbledon, The Open, The Super Bowl, cup finals, rugby internationals, snooker finals, darts championships – you've won the lot. Sport enriches your life and you love to read and to hear about the exploits of those who just happen to have been born with more talent.

Whoever you are, this appeal is for you.

What we Christians believe is that God created man, and as the preacher says, "when we talk about man we embrace woman". We may disagree about how He created mankind, but all Christians acknowledge the hand of God can be detected in the things which He has made. That is what the Bible teaches. Further, we know that God created with a purpose. His was not the random creation of the production line. "Let us run with patience the particular race that God has set before us" is how the Living Bible paraphrases the beginning of Hebrews 12.

God created each one of us, superstar, club hacker or armchair critic, for a purpose. When He gave us "sport" He gave it for a reason. There is a race marked out, a plan for our lives which we do well to discover and follow. Sport is part of that plan for us.

Eric Liddell was a man who discovered the joy of running the race. Initially for him it was a literal race – he won a gold medal in the 1924 Olympics, and his life has been vividly recalled in the Oscar-winning film, *Chariots of Fire*. Later "the race" involved missionary work in China. Whether it was as an athlete or as a missionary eventually dying in China, Eric ran with persevering faith, bringing joy and comfort and hope to all who knew him and setting an example of Christian manliness for subsequent generations.

Eric, though supremely talented, was in other ways no different from the rest of us. But he heard the loud appeal and responded.

Christians proclaim a God who created us and loves us, accepting us for what we are. But it is not just that. Our God has come to us in the person of Jesus Christ, His Son. He is with us each day and longs for us to get our lives in step with Him.

There is no part of our lives which will not be immeasurably better if it is lived the Jesus way . . . and that includes sport.

In this book I have told the story of many Christians in sport who have responded like Eric Liddell did and, playing with abandonment and commitment, have experienced God's pleasure.

That is not to say that it will always be easy. Gene Mayer rose to be the fourth-best tennis player in the world behind Borg, McEnroe and Connors in the early 1980s. He was a delicate mid-court player, skill factor playing a vital part in his game. Early in his career Gene began to learn what it really meant to trust God. I met him in Indianapolis. He said, "I acknowledged before God that my tennis was His . . . all my relationships, even the way I drive my car, are His. The whole idea is this, I think; to have a godly perspective and to seek to understand what He wants us to do. That outlook is essential in all the things I do."

Inevitably Gene got criticised in the media for not being intense. His relaxed manner contrasted markedly with the total absorption with the games of the illustrious trio ahead of him in the merit table. Stan Smith said of him, "Gene is the most frustrating player for me to play on tour and that includes Borg, Connors and McEnroe. He can keep you off-balance so much with his change of direction, change of speed and change of angle, better than anyone else." And *Sports Illustrated* agreed. "No one in the game has a better variety of shots."

Yet No. 4 was the best Gene became. Why? He explains.

In order to have possibly been No. 1 in the world, it would have taken a rearrangement of my priorities, which I am not willing to do . . . first, having a relationship with God that is healthy, then, having a healthy relationship with my family, and then to think of tennis as my occupation.

But then No. 4 isn't bad, is it?

Mayer had decided that he needed to be God's man before all else. In his case that meant not being the world's leading tennis player.

For others it has been different. Julius Erving (Dr J.) was for many years, without question, the hottest property in world basketball – a totally committed Christian. Indonesian Rudi Hartono won the world badminton championships an unprecedented seven times. I met Rudi in Hong Kong, when he was quite a young Christian. Knowing very little about badminton, I knew nothing of this legend within the game. But his quiet strength and integrity greatly impressed me.

A few years later I attended the all-England badminton championships at Wembley. I asked a friend in the England team which of the Indonesians were Christians.

"Well, most of them, I think," came the answer. "It all began with Hartono, you know."

We sat down by the court side and watched a beautifully athletic Indonesian lady winning a doubles match.

"Who's that?" I asked.

"Imelda Kurniawan, Rudi's sister-in-law."

"Is she a Christian?"

"I think so. Would you like to meet her?"

After the match I was duly introduced as a minister working with sportspeople. Imelda's face shone with delight.

"You were praying?" she asked in faltering English, smiling all over her lovely face.

I hesitated. I do not believe in praying to win. Why should God particularly want me, or Imelda, or anybody else to win? But, as Christians do, I had certainly been praying that we would meet and be able to encourage one another. On balance I decided to say yes.

"Jesus played every shot," was Imelda's giggling reply. I suppose some would be cynical about such an attitude. But to me it was a shining example of what it means to be using your talent the Jesus way. Imelda did not mean she had an unfair advantage. I don't suppose Jesus was a great badminton player, anyway, though I expect He could fashion a handy racket in his carpenter's shop. No, she knew the Lord's presence with her, she had surrendered her life, including her great talent for badminton to Him and so all of her life was inseparably and permanently linked with Him.

It's not always easy combining Christian faith of this depth and sincerity with the competitiveness required in top-level sport. Tommy Curren was ranked in the best top six surfers in the world in 1984/85 at the tender age of twenty-one. He is California's prime hope of a world title. He says:

Christianity affects my outlook on life, and surfing is just one aspect of my life. I believe the best surfer – the one who trains the hardest and demonstrates the most talent – should win contests, not the one who prays to win. I don't think God supports that attitude any way. That would be completely unfair – if God chose someone to win a race over someone else.

Cricketer Alan Knott in his autobiography, *It's Knott Cricket*, makes a similar point.

Let the result take care of itself. That is the healthiest attitude for a cricketer. Many players become so involved in the result that nerves take over. You should accept that cricket is a game which sometimes you will lose. I try not to mind whether we lose or win. The only time I would get upset is if I felt I had not tried hard enough. If you have tried your utmost and things still didn't go right for you, there's nothing you can do about it.

What a difference it will make to our country, even to our world, when more and more sportsmen and sportswomen commit their lives to Jesus Christ. This is my loud appeal – to call all who love sport and derive great pleasure from it, back to the God who ultimately provides the pleasure. We have such a privilege in having minds and bodies that work. Top-level performances receive the adulations of millions, and with the pleasure and privilege comes responsibility.

Role models

During 1986 sport was continually in the headlines. A famous cricketer was banned for two months for allegations concerning drugs; a Welsh rugby international was banned for assaulting an opponent; another rugby player was heavily fined for biting an opponent's ear off; the Commonwealth Games were boycotted for political reasons; English football clubs remained isolated from European competitions because of repeated barbaric acts of hooliganism by so-called supporters; a former world snooker champion was prosecuted for assaulting a tournament official; endless stories of "drug, drinks and sex orgies" involving the England cricket team in the Caribbean filled the "Sundays".

There was the usual round of management sackings. At Somerset County Cricket Club a major row broke out over the club's decision not to renew the contracts of two great West Indian players, Richards and Garner, who had been playing for Somerset for ten years. Only after a special general meeting was the committee's decision upheld.

Manchester United Football Club disposed of their manager, Ron Atkinson, while across the road at Lancashire County Cricket Club, manager Jack Bond – of the Madras healing service fame – led his side to Lord's, lost the Nat-West final in a close game with Sussex and was promptly "fired" next morning.

Behind every one of these incidents – and there were many others – there is a human story of pain and sorrow. Individuals are deeply affected by their achievements in sport and by the media coverage of their lives.

But with what image are our young people being presented? Do caring parents see sport as promoting the ideals and standards they want for their children? Like it or not, sportsmen and sportswomen have great influence. TV and media coverage exaggerate their successes and their failures on and off the playing area. The men and women who play at top level influence the way many others in society behave.

Yet who cares for these men and women? Who helps them to be the kind of people we want our children to emulate? I long that they should know the love and concern of Christian people, and come to see that life does not consist of success in sport, but in a vibrant, positive relationship with God.

The stories of Graham Barlow and Justin Fashanu illustrate the points I am making.

"Fash"

Justin Fashanu was a Dr Barnardo's boy. His parents came from Guyana, but he was eventually fostered by an English family in Norfolk. He signed apprentice forms with Norwich City and by the age of seventeen was a regular in the "Canaries" 1st team, winning six England under-21 caps. On February 9th, 1980, Norwich played Liverpool at Carrow Road and Justin scored a sensational goal, turning and firing the ball into the top left-hand corner of the net from thirty yards out. That goal won the "goal of the season" contest on BBC television and made Justin a million-pound footballer. That was the fee that the controversial Nottingham Forest manager, Brian Clough, paid for this sensational youngster in August 1981.

Life was as good as it could be for big Justin. At the age of eighteen he had achieved fame and fortune as a footballer . . . but yet he felt strangely empty.

He was living in a hotel suite with everything provided, including a sponsored car. It was in connection with the latter that he went to Terry Gibson's garage in Nottingham.

"Are you happy, Justin?" was Terry's surprising question.

Justin thought he must be happy. He was well known, pampered, rich, glamorous, sought-after and successful.

"No." he replied.

Four hours later Justin and Terry knelt together in the sale-room of the garage and Justin answered the loud appeal, and said yes to God.

Justin responded at the very peak of his career. Since

then he has had problems. He never settled at Forest and was transferred to Notts County and eventually Brighton. There a knee injury which had been plaguing him for years grew worse and put his whole future as a player at risk.

Like Richie Powling before him, Justin's world was caving in . . . and yet it wasn't. The Bible teaches us that "in all things God works for the good of those who love him" (Romans 8:28). Justin absolutely believes in this. He has learnt things about God and himself that he would not have learnt any other way. He is a proud, self-confident man, conscious of his good looks and athletic appearance. But he has been brought low, humbled, by this injury. Yet Justin Fashanu of 1987 is a more "refined", more "whole" human being than the 1980 model.

He is still the same man, charming, witty, intelligent, maddeningly unreliable, and then disarmingly charming about it, but he is God's man and it is plain for all to see.

Soon after Justin was transferred to Brighton, he decided to stop playing on Sundays and informed the club that he would not be available for selection on the Lord's day.

"But why, Justin?" I asked. "It has not worried you before. God has given you the talent for His glory – I don't suppose He minds terribly which day you play on."

I was being deliberately provocative. Sunday sport is, of course, a major problem for many Christians in Great Britain. I don't feel particularly strongly about it, but share all Christians' preference for not playing on a Sunday so that church attendance and involvement, as well as family commitment, can be maintained.

"I feel I should be with the Lord's people on Sundays," he replied. "We might still be able to stop Sunday football on a large scale, and I want to contribute to that."

"OK, but why decide now?" I asked. "What brought the decision on?"

"Well I did play the last two Sunday games . . . and I got sent off both times! Do you think the Lord is trying to tell me something?"

I will long remember an evening in Hull Rugby League Club when Justin and I were addressing a fairly down-to-earth group of Humbersiders. Justin had crutches, a blackboard, chalk, a Bible and a firm grasp of what Christianity is all about.

"I'll draw you a few pictures," he said in his unmistakably southern accent, "'cos I know you are all a bit thick up here!" They loved it and him and listened intently as he gave the loud appeal.

Graham Barlow

I first met Graham in 1971 when he was playing for the English universities and I was in the Oxford side. He was already a prolific free-scoring left-hand bat, contracted to Middlesex County Cricket Club. For the following fifteen years he was a key figure in a marvellous Middlesex team that won all the honours going in the game. He toured India with the England team and played in the Centenary Test Match against Australia at Lord's. His personal life was less successful than his playing career. Two wives came and went, and by 1984 his career was threatened by a degenerative back and hip injury.

Coaching in South Africa, he met and married Kenau, a mature, down-to-earth South African lecturer in languages. Kenau had also been married and had a teenage daughter. Her first husband had experienced a dramatic conversion to Christianity soon after their divorce and Kenau was very suspicious of the "religious fanaticism" which, as she saw it, he exhibited. But she had a firm faith herself, springing from her Christian upbringing. It seemed to her a personal and private matter, and the enthusiasm of "born-again" Christians antagonised her.

In early summer 1986 Graham and Kenau were

together in England. She was pregnant, the baby expected in September. Graham's injury was rapidly deteriorating and in June his body was sealed in a plaster cast and he had to wait for six weeks and hope for healing. During that time he talked to several Christian people, began to read the Bible and other Christian literature which his friends provided.

It was all quite new to Graham. Kenau knew what Christianity was all about, but perhaps because of Graham's excitement she came at it fresh.

As his professional life fell apart, Graham was finding a new and much greater security in the "reality" of his relationship with Kenau, and the expectation of a baby, and in God. The Bible seemed to make sense to him, and he liked what he saw in the lives of the Christians he knew. In September, soon after Gede was born, they knelt in a minister's study in North London and gave their lives to Christ. Graham rang me that evening.

"We've committed our lives to Christ," he announced joyfully. "It's great!"

Coming to Christ gave Graham what he describes in his own words as "a real sense of values and a code to live by, which was totally missing in my life up until then".

In due course it became clear that professional cricket was out for Graham from then on. His back did not heal and Middlesex signed him off. At the end-of-season party no mention was made of G. D. Barlow – fifteen years of his life gone and not a word of thanks!

One should not particularly blame Middlesex. Professional sport is about money. Unhealthy, out-of-form players do not earn money. Indeed it can cost a great deal to get them fit again. The inevitable emphasis in top-class sport is on the physical aspect of human existence – every club has at least a doctor and a physiotherapist. There is a growing awareness of the need for the right mental attitude and the whole science of sports psychology is emerging. But the essence of man, his spiritual life, has been sadly neglected; indeed, often it is sneered at.

Strength is understood to be demonstrated by the macho, "Rambo"- style sportsman; the big kid who never grows up, but who starts playing with real people's lives instead of toy Action Men.

There are numerous casualties in a world of such topsy-turvy values. Often they are the wives and children, but we all know of and have read about the boxer who ends up in the gutter and the footballer hooked on gambling. There is probably no rugby club in the country that has not got its share of "old boys" whose meaning in life revolves around Saturday afternoon at the club bar.

God intended life to be much more than this. Jesus said "I have come in order that you may have life – life in all its fullness" (John 10:10 GN). The Bible often contrasts God's offer of life with the living death which people without Christ experience. Many people involved in sport eventually reach the point – usually during the "morning after the night before" – where they cry, "There must be something more than this!"

The wonderful, thrilling, unchanging truth is that there is. Jesus Christ is alive today and offers us His quality of life which He lived. He offers us a lasting, meaningful relationship with God. He offers forgiveness for everything we have done – a clean sheet. He offers us His spirit, who will be with us, in us, enabling us to overcome, slowly perhaps but successfully the habits and sins which dog our footsteps today.

Millions of people around the world know and experience the truth of what I have written . . . but before you decide, read the next chapter.

8

The Umpire's Decision

It was a glorious, sunny June day. The blossom from the trees and the pretty girls in their long dresses floated across the university Parks in Oxford. Along the river undergraduates, champagned and relieved at the end of their final exams, poled their punts past Parson's Pleasure.

The flannelled fools of the university team, among whom I was numbered, failed to foil the menace of a county attack. Worcestershire beat us again. It seemed no big deal. We always lost, anyway. This was the last match in Oxford. That evening the team would be announced and should all disappear on tour for two weeks before the climax of the season, the gladiatorial contest with Cambridge at Lord's.

I had other reasons for believing that all was well with the world. My finals were over, and to my amazement, and that of my tutor, I was on course for a decent degree. I was in love. Sue and I had our tickets for the Christ Church May Ball that evening, and it would be an evening of fun and laughter with our friends. With two other friends I was planning an overland trek to East Africa where I was due to work with the Church Missionary Society for two years. There was no need to think about that till September . . . and the summer stretched ahead.

The captain sat himself down beside me on the pavilion seats.

"Andrew, could I have a word? We have decided to leave you out of the side, I'm afraid."

"But that's ridiculous – I did so well last year, and I have had only one game since finals; I will be bowling very well by the time of the Varsity match . . ."

"I'm sorry . . . that's our decision."

"But – "

'I'm sorry, you'd better collect your things!"

There was nothing more to be said. What I thought was irrelevant. My fate was decided by others. My world, so perfect a few minutes before, collapsed.

In Cambridge the system is even harder. On the morning of the team's announcement, the captain cycles round to all those involved. For some it is congratulations, and for some, "I'm sorry, we have to leave you out." In such a situation it is no good protesting that you are the best player in the team, or that the captain hates your guts, or that he fancies your girlfriend, or that he's Welsh . . . you are not selected and there is absolutely nothing you can do about it.

The same experience can happen during play. Involved in a minor fracas, as it seems to you, in which the other man was the instigator, the referee shows you the red card.

"Come on, ref, he poked me in the eye!"

"Off!" the crowd start shouting or barking, if you played rugby at my level. The game's over for you – it's the early bath.

You bowl for over after over, working at a batsman's weakness, looking for the chink in his armour. Finally you trap him right in front of all three stumps.

"Howzat?"

"Not out." And the umpire turns his back on you . . . sometimes he smiles!

What sportsman or sportswoman has not been robbed . . .

"I never touched him, ref" . . . "He was offside, ref" . . . "That pass was forward, ref" . . . "I never hit it, umpire."

You can hardly watch a tennis match at Wimbledon without the linesman or umpire making a vital decision. There is hardly a sport which is without its disputed incidents. The contestants are in the hands of the legitimate authorities – their decision is final.

What is true of sport is true of life, too.

God is the ruler of this world. He made it. He sustains it by His power. He lays down the rules of existence and the standards by which men and women should live. As the king and ruler, what He says goes. He is absolute in the exercise of His authority.

He chose, the Bible teaches us, to make man and woman and to delegate the day-to-day running of the world to them. He gave man "dominion" over all created things, and invested in man the right to rule (Gen. 1:26). As John wrote in the Book of Revelation, "You, Lord and God . . . created all things, and by your will they were given existence" (Rev. 4:11 GN).

The trouble is, of course, that we all reject God's authority over us. We want to run our own lives our own way without God. Never is this more evident than in sport. We recognise that our talent comes from elsewhere. After all, however arrogant we are, we can claim no part in the way we are put together; the fact that we have an eye for a ball, or have the physical attributes to run fast. These are "given things". But, ironically, it is our love for, and ability at, sport that we often hold on to most tightly.

"It's my thing. It's how I relax, unwind. I don't know what I'd do if I didn't have my squash."

Of course, in the area of morality our failure to accept God's authority is even more disastrous. We find we can control neither ourselves nor the society in which we live. In our personal lives we fail again and again to live up to our own standards, let alone God's. And in our global and national life we store up more and more for ourselves so that others go hungry and starve. We misuse our sexual desires, so that sex, which God

gave us to be both enjoyable in itself and a fun way of procreating, becomes a weapon we use against each other and a means of spreading disease and unhappiness.

Paul put it very candidly in his letter to the Christians in Rome: "All have sinned and fall short of the glory of God" (Rom. 3:23 RSV). Sin then is a rejection of God's authority; the symptoms of this rebellion are what we commonly refer to as "sins" – stealing, lying, blaspheming, sexual immorality, drunkenness, murder and so on. We may not be into the more exotic of these pastimes, but all of us have, to one degree or another, rejected God's authority. Jesus said "You shall love the Lord your God with all your heart, and with all your soul, and with all your mind and with all your strength" (Mark 12:30 RSV). Well, none of us has done that, have we?

The problem is that God is the great umpire, the great referee and the great selector. What will He do about our rebellion?

Consider this example for a moment: I find most sportspeople pretty intolerant of terrorism. They rightly regard it as both a barbaric and cowardly way of waging war. Suppose there was a terrorist bomb in your

town, killing and maiming innocent people. Suppose
you had the authority in your town to dispense
justice to the perpetrators of this crime when they were
caught. Would you let them off or would you punish
them? Cricketer Ian Botham went on television to say
that he thought all heroin-pushers should be hung.
That may be untypically ruthless, but I suspect most
sportsmen would have little sympathy for a convicted
bomber.

We are terrorists in God's world. He will not allow us
to continue to rebel against Him. His punishment for
rebellion is eternal death. You may find this part of my
book very hard to stomach, but we all need to know what
the decision of the great referee is:

"OFF!"

". . . Those who do not know God and do not obey the
gospel of our Lord Jesus . . . will be punished with
everlasting destruction and shut out from the presence of
the Lord" (2 Thess. 1:8–9 NIV).

"NOT SELECTED!"

Because I am writing to fellow sports enthusiasts I
refuse to water this down. We should understand that if
we are not good enough for the team then we are not
selected. If we infringe the rules then we are punished.
That is the way of sport and that is the way of God's
dealing with the human race.

"IT IS FAIR."

But, and please read on, we have a God who is not fair.
His love overrules. Because of His love God sent his Son
into our world – the man Jesus Christ. Jesus was flesh
and blood just like you and me. No doubt he played in
the streets with the other kids. He had sexual drives just
like we do. He felt the need to compete and win just like
we do. But He was God. He lived always under God's
rule. He did not rebel; He did not become a terrorist. He
alone, of all the millions who have walked this planet,
did not sin.

Jesus came to take our punishment for us, by dying in

our place. His greatest friend, Peter, who accompanied Him for three years, who played in His team, bathed and changed with Him, sweated and toiled with Him, wrote, "He committed no sin . . . He himself bore our sins in his body on the tree" (1 Pet. 1:22, 24 NIV). Sportsmen know only too well that nobody is perfect. Even the greatest players sometimes make mistakes on the field. Even the most saintly and unselfish of people sometimes slip up, but Peter says Jesus never did, and he would have known.

Like terrorists, we deserved punishment, eternal destruction, but Jesus stepped into our shoes and was punished in our place. God's love was so great that He provided the solution to the problem of man's rebellion. Grasp this and you are beginning to know what life is all about.

Forgive me a feeble sporting illustration: I was driving down the M4 in England listening to Second Division Oxford United playing Everton in a crucial cup-tie. Oxford were 1-0 up with five minutes to go . . . a huge cup upset was in the offing. I was struggling to keep my hands on the steering-wheel! With a few minutes left an Oxford defender, no doubt trying to waste time, passed the ball back towards his goalkeeper. But the pass lacked pace. Adrian Heath, that nippy Everton striker, ran on to the ball, rounded the goalkeeper and slammed it into the back of the net; 1-1 the final score. Everton won the replay.

When all seemed lost, when there was no hope of victory for Everton, Oxford presented them with a goal. The ball was laid at Heath's feet and all he had to do was score – a gift goal.

The cross of Jesus Christ, if I may say so reverently, is the ultimate back-pass in cosmic history. God has laid the ball at our feet. He has done all that He possibly could to give us the chance of winning and we just have to score.

But that is not all. God raised Jesus to life again. The

death and destruction which we all justly face could not destroy Jesus. He rose again, conquering death, proving that He is the ruler of the world for He rules with ultimate power. He is alive today to give new life to all who will receive it.

Perhaps you say, "I could never believe that a dead man walked again." I'm not asking you to believe it as a matter of course. It happened only once in history and it will never happen in quite the same way again. A man of flesh and blood died in agony on a Roman gallows and after two nights in a tomb was raised to life. He never died again and is alive today.

Numerous books have been written on this subject and I strongly encourage any doubters to examine the evidence for themselves . . . but consider just these indisputable facts:

1. The tomb was empty.
2. No one ever produced the body.
3. Numerous independent witnesses claimed they saw, spoke and ate with the risen Jesus. Their lives were permanently changed by their experience of this.
4. For nearly 2,000 years the number of people who claim to have met the risen Jesus has grown to millions and millions in every country on this planet. Can they all be wrong?

Peter, that same friend who wrote about Jesus's sinless life was a pretty down-to-earth fellow – a fisherman from Galilee, a rural area in northern Palestine. These days Peter would have been a second-row forward, or a winchman in a 12-metre yacht, or a shot-putter . . . anyway, not the sort to invent stories about the dead being raised. But Peter said in the very first Christian sermon, "God has raised this Jesus to life, and we are all witnesses of the fact" (Acts 2:32 NIV). And then years later, when you might have expected the first flush of enthusiasm to be wearing off, he wrote "In his great mercy he has given us new birth into a living hope through the resurrection of Jesus Christ from the dead" (1 Peter 1:3 NIV).

So the umpire's decision on your life and mine was "guilty" but "forgiven". It is not that our foul has been overlooked. The whistle has gone and we are in trouble, but just as you head for the changing-room, the captain steps in and says, "My fault, ref, I'll go off." You know it was not the captain's fault, but you also know that he wants you to go on playing.

This can actually happen in cricket. Imagine yourself in a run out mix-up with the captain and star batsman at the other end. You make a muddle of the calling and end up at the captain's end – a run out is inevitable. But to your amazement the captain who was totally innocent of the muddle in the first place sacrifices his wicket and wishes you well as he leaves the scene.

In the light of God's action what will we do? It has been said that there are really just two ways to live.

You can continue to reject God's authority, insisting on running your own life your own way. Such a choice is respected by God, but you are then responsible for this decision and your actions based on it. You will condemn yourself and will face eternal death. You would, I imagine, expect nothing else.

Or you can submit to Jesus's authority, relying on His death and Resurrection as the method of receiving forgiveness and new life which will last for ever.

As you finish this book let me ask you straight. "Which of these represents the way you want to live?"

If you choose to submit to Jesus, you will be born again, given a completely new start, the Spirit of Jesus will come and live in your heart. You will not have to change overnight, although you will have to want to be changed. The Holy Spirit working quietly but powerfully will begin to do His work.

This is what you must do; ask God to forgive you and

change you. Tell Him that you are going to rely entirely on Jesus for your forgiveness and on His Spirit to give new life. Submit yourself unreservedly to Jesus as your ruler.

Here's a prayer you could use:

Dear God, I know I am not worthy to be called a child of God. I don't deserve your gift of eternal life. I am guilty of rebelling against you and ignoring you. I need forgiveness.

Thank you for sending Jesus, your Son, to die for me that I may be forgiven. Thank you that you raised Him to give me new life. Please forgive me and change me that I may live with Jesus as my Lord and master – Amen.

Oh, and one more thing. Could you write to me and tell me what you've decided. I'd love to help you further.

Christians in Sport
PO Box 93
Oxford OX1 1QX